Inspiring Early Childhood Leadership

Eight Strategies to Ignite Passion and Transform Program Quality

Susan MacDonald

Gryphon House
Award-Winning Publisher of
Early Childhood Resources

Published by Gryphon House, Inc.

P. O. Box 10, Lewisville, NC 27023

800.638.0928; 877.638.7576 (fax)

Visit us on the web at www.gryphonhouse.com.

Bulk Purchase

Gryphon House books are available for special premiums and sales promotions as well as for fund-raising use. Special editions or book excerpts also can be created to specifications. For details, call 800.638.0928.

Disclaimer

Gryphon House, Inc., cannot be held responsible for damage, mishap, or injury incurred during the use of or because of activities in this book. Appropriate and reasonable caution and adult supervision of children involved in activities and corresponding to the age and capability of each child involved are recommended at all times. Do not leave children unattended at any time. Observe safety and caution at all times.

Privacy Statement

All of the stories of leaders are authentic; the names of people and organizations have been changed to preserve the privacy and business confidentiality.

Library of Congress Cataloging-in-Publication Data

Names: MacDonald, Susan, 1961 June 14-

Title: Inspiring early childhood leadership : eight strategies to ignite
   passion and transform program quality / Susan MacDonald.

Description: Lewisville, NC : Gryphon House, 2016.

Identifiers: LCCN 2016027997 | ISBN 9780876596517

Subjects: LCSH: Early childhood education--United States.

Classification: LCC LB1139.25 .M33 2016 | DDC 372.21--dc23 LC record available at
   https://lccn.loc.gov/2016027997

Dedication

To my mother, whose commitment to providing unconditional love to the hundreds of children who were blessed to spend their days in her care provided the foundation for my ongoing passion for creating strengths-based environments for children to thrive in.

Dorothy Elizabeth MacDonald holding Susan Elizabeth MacDonald.

Contents

Introduction

This book explores how leaders can find new and empowering ways to adapt to the evolving world of early childhood education. Research into the immense, lifelong value of education at this stage of development has created a wave of reforms designed to increase the quality of early childhood programs. The research and its many resulting initiatives are aligned with the field's long-standing commitment to provide quality education and care to all children.

The field of early childhood education is at a crossroads. On one path is the current research that documents the vital importance of high-quality learning environments for young children. Down the second path are the ideas and practices that have been pervasive in the early childhood field for decades. Today's leaders of early childhood programs are faced with a multitude of questions:

- How do I motivate and inspire teachers?

- How can I be more effective in observing and giving nonjudgmental feedback?

- How can I be more confident in my role as a leader?

- How can I manage my time more effectively?

- How can I keep up with and help teachers align their programs with the newly articulated standards and quality initiatives without being overwhelmed and adding to the stress my teachers feel?

Inspiring Early Childhood Leadership is the reflection of the insights cultivated through my rich professional experiences supporting quality in early childhood programs. Throughout my career, I have supported these programs in many different ways—as a coach, consultant, professional speaker, college instructor, licensing supervisor, and director of a Reggio-inspired preschool. In each of these roles, I was able to see the stresses and challenges of truly creating a supportive, educational, and vibrant learning community. Over the years I have designed and delivered a myriad of leadership courses focused on supporting early childhood directors in reenergizing their programs, embracing change, and aligning with new standards and initiatives. I have seen firsthand the negative impact that stress can have on the culture and climate of a program. I have been inspired to write this book to support directors in moving past their challenges and envisioning new possibilities for creating high-quality learning environments fueled by positive, engaging energy.

The goal of this book is to help you tap into the energy, passion, and engagement needed to truly lead early childhood programs. All too often, the words I hear from directors describing their energy for their work include *overwhelmed, stressed, exhausted, flat out,* or *drowning.* These are key descriptors for a negative spiral. Leading from a place of low energy and negativity increases the challenges for directors and makes strengths-based program transformation impossible. The strategies laid out in this book are designed to support directors in finding new ways to reduce the levels of stress and move into a unified, engaging system for leading with passion, intention, and purpose.

This shift from overwhelmed to focused, engaged leadership is truly what facilitates quality transformations. I have seen the shift many times in the directors that I work with in leadership groups and as coaching clients. One of the most vivid examples of moving from a point of overwhelming negativity into a fully engaged and inspirational leadership role is my encounter with Lyn. When I met Lyn, at the first session of a five-part Directing with Vision and Clarity course, I thought she had mistakenly come into the wrong room. The course was being held at a community college and Lyn's appearance—sullen expression, head down, wearing a sweatshirt with the hood up—made her appear much more like a disgruntled college student than the leader of an early childhood program.

After Lyn introduced herself to the group, two things were evident: she was in the right place, and she was in a crisis of leadership. When she shared her journey to her leadership position, it was inspiring. Lyn had quickly moved from being an assistant teacher to becoming a director who purchased the program and the building from the school's founder. Her focus and drive had helped her achieve her dream of running and owning the program. However, that focus and drive had eroded under the stresses she felt as she faced staff challenges, new Quality Rating Improvement System (QRIS) requirements, and an overwhelming sense of low energy across the program. On that first day of the course, Lyn shared with the group that she was seriously considering tossing aside her dream of running a high-quality early program and selling the school. Lyn wasn't just in a negative spiral; she was at the very bottom of the energy vortex. Although the course had more than twenty participants, the heavy drained energy that Lyn brought was permeating the whole classroom.

The focus for this first session was for each participant to write a vision statement that reflected their hopes, dreams, and aspirations as a leader in their program. Somehow, just thinking about all that was possible began to create a subtle shift in Lyn's demeanor. Her hood came off, and she volunteered to share her vision with the group. In that vision was the hope for the future that would guide Lyn into fully embracing her dreams for herself as a positive inspirational leader and her vision for all that her program could be.

The journey up the spiral was not always easy for Lyn. She faced challenges and setbacks, but she stuck with her vision and developed a clear action plan for achieving her goals. Lyn became acutely aware of how her energy was reflected throughout the program, and she refused to let setbacks push her back down into the negative spiral. Her focus on staying true to her vision allowed her to implement many changes that have enhanced her program and her confidence in her own leadership abilities.

Lyn now speaks nationally about her leadership transformation and inspires others to shift to strengths-based leadership! Working closely with her and many other leaders in similar low-energy states has been my inspiration for writing this book. The strategies you will find here are designed to help you customize your own journey to increase your engagement and passion for the vitally important work of leading early childhood programs.

The key premise of *Inspiring Early Childhood Leadership* is that a positive, strengths-based leadership system is the key to transforming quality in early childhood programs. Across the field it is evident that the stress of leading early childhood programs is on the rise. Increasing demands from the many new quality initiatives and standards have contributed to feelings of work pressure and have drained directors' and teachers' energy, creating school communities where low levels of engagement have become the norm. When engagement is low, all aspects of the program suffer, and the children feel these negative effects strongly.

The research is clear that high-quality early childhood programs have a lasting impact on the lives of children and families. In a 2014 article in *Time* magazine, Fareed Zakaria notes that the Organisation of Economic Co-operation and Development has found that early-childhood education "improves children's cognitive abilities, helps to create a foundation for lifelong learning, makes learning outcomes more equitable, reduces poverty and improves social mobility from generation to generation." Research findings like this have fueled a new sense of urgency at the national political level, which is building the momentum needed to bring about much-needed, lasting changes for early childhood programs. The time to fully commit to increasing the effectiveness of your program is now.

Inspiring Early Childhood Leadership lays out eight clear strategies that will support the development of vibrant learning communities where all teachers, children, and parents can thrive. This system aligns current research on positive psychology, school transformation, and strengths-based leadership with the current standards of quality in the early childhood field. This alignment creates new insights into what is needed to strengthen early childhood programs through consistent, intentional, and supportive leadership.

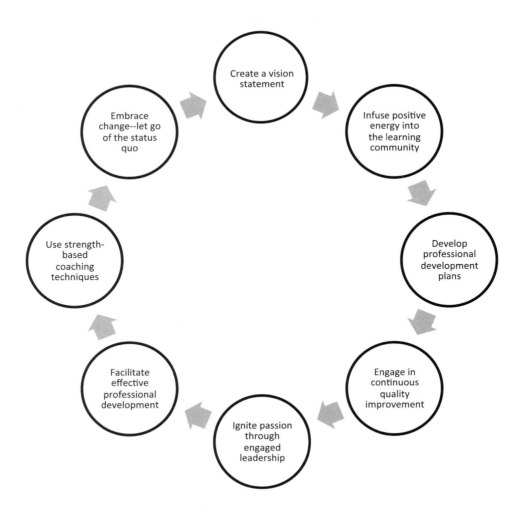

Eight Strategies for Igniting Passion and Engagement in Early Childhood Programs

The journey to transform your early childhood program requires commitment and the intention to fully engage in the reflective practice exercises throughout this book. Bringing to life your vision for all that your program can be is a richly rewarding experience that leads to higher levels of professional satisfaction for all administrators and teachers. It also creates a vibrant learning community where children will develop the skills needed for success.

Quality early childhood education is vitally important and directly linked to children's success throughout school—indeed, during their entire lives. Providing a strong foundation in the early years is essential to the development of strong social and intellectual skills. In President Barack Obama's State of the Union address on February 12, 2013, he clearly stated the long-term benefits of quality early childhood education:

"In states that make it a priority to educate our youngest children . . . studies show students grow up more likely to read and do math at grade level, graduate high school, hold a job, form more stable families of their own. We know this works. So let's do what works and make sure none of our children start the race of life already behind."

In the United States, quality initiatives have received billions of dollars in federal funding. Quality rating systems are being established in all fifty states. Each rating system is unique, but their fundamental focus is the same: supporting high-quality care for young children. In addition to the new QRIS initiatives, program leaders are adapting to new regulations and changing accreditation standards. All of these modifications are designed to create the quality learning environments children need. Embracing the programmatic changes required in early childhood programs calls for a new supportive system of leadership. The strategies laid out in this book are instrumental to developing the leadership skills necessary to support programs as they move from the status quo up the energy spiral to a place where full engagement and passion for the important work of early childhood programs flourish.

Incorporating these new quality initiatives into manageable systems for program leadership and staff supervision can be a struggle. School leaders are trying to juggle all the quality-related balls, while at the same time trying to balance the many leadership hats they are wearing.

Just like the peddler in the classic children's book *Caps for Sale,* directors are always trying to balance their many, many hats. This is a difficult feat in the best of times, but when you add in the many unexpected challenges of leading in ever-changing times, many directors are unsure if they will ever be able to create a sense of balance and calm in their programs.

Source: Illustrations copyright © 1940 and 1947 Esphyr Slobodkina. Copyright renewed 1968 by Esphyr Slobodkina. Used by permission of HarperCollins Publishers.

Inspiring Early Childhood Leadership will guide you on your journey to develop a system that will ignite passion, engagement, and intention into all aspects of your program. You will begin by creating a vision statement that reflects all that your program could be, and then you will move through specific strategies and reflective practice exercises that will support and guide you as you bring your vision to life.

I think of vision as the light at the end of the tunnel. After working with a program leader in a coaching relationship for a few months, I noticed a new spark of energy as she talked about her program. For years she had been struggling with being overwhelmed by accreditation standards, licensing requirements, and the new quality rating scale the state was implementing. I wanted to know more about this new vibrant energy I observed, so I asked her if "the light at the end of the tunnel" had turned on for her. After a moment of reflection she replied "No, all the lights in the tunnel have turned on!" She described a sense of joy and relief when she realized that all the initiatives were directly linked to her own vision to create a high-quality program where children thrive and teachers happily engage in all aspects of their work. She was able to see for the first time how aligning with the new initiatives and integrating them into her daily work to bring her vision to life could transform her program.

My hope is that you will experience that electrifying moment when all the lights in the tunnel come on, when you as a leader step into the light and reenergize yourself and your programs to provide the high-quality early childhood care and education that children and families so desperately need.

CHAPTER 1

Creating a Collaborative Vision Statement

Oh, it's delightful to have ambitions. I'm so glad I have such a lot. And there never seems to be any end to them—that's the best of it. Just as soon as you attain to one ambition you see another one glittering higher up still. It does make life so interesting.

—L. M. Montgomery, *Anne of Green Gables*

Naturally, directors aspire to create high-quality early childhood programs. Yet many leaders are caught up in the struggle to get through each day and give little thought or energy to the big-picture vision for their program. Early childhood directors tend to be overly busy and often feel unsatisfied with their professional accomplishments. Directing an early childhood program without a clear vision and a system for leading your program can leave you feeling physically tired, stressed, and professionally drained. Why? Because when you lack a compelling vision statement and clear goals to guide your actions, you fill your days going through the motions and tackling the crisis du jour. This leads to wasted energy, an increased sense of frustration, and low levels of engagement. Working with a well-defined vision statement will support you in moving from being busy at work to being fully engaged, focused, and productive in your work.

A compelling vision statement is essential to creating a journey of growth for your program. Developing your vision with input from teachers, parents, and board members will build the collaboration that is essential for programwide transformation. A vision statement, quite simply, paints a vibrant picture of your program operating at its highest level of success. Each program will define *success* in different ways, and that process works best with input from all the stakeholders.

A Method to Your Madness

Vision statements are not a new approach to education. They have been used for centuries to inspire and guide the work of individuals and institutions. I often reflect on this old proverb: "A vision without a plan is just a dream. A plan without a vision is drudgery. But a vision with a plan can change the world." In the early childhood field, many programs are working without a vision or a plan that will support bringing the vision to life. Meg, a participant in a Wheelock College Leadership Course I taught, described the importance of creating a vision statement and action plan in this way: "My vision has always been clear to me, but the process of writing it out with a timeline and being detailed and thoughtful about how to get where I want to be was a wonderful process. I feel I have always worked to implement my vision, but there was no real method to my madness. Having this plan helps me to feel that my goals can be accomplished."

Meg's thoughts capture the importance of not just having a vision but having goals that can be implemented to create the reality described in the vision statement. Moving from the vision being a dream to being a guiding light for the work of the director and teachers is essential for transformation to take place. In the book *Soul Mission, Life Vision*, Alan Seale describes how a clear vision can guide our daily work: "Vision gives us hope, direction, and a path to follow. In times of a crisis, it is vision of another possibility that helps us through. And in everyday living, it is vision that keeps us on track, engaged in the creation of a positive, purposeful, and rewarding life." The power and importance of having a collaborative vision statement cannot be understated. It is the essential first step in the journey to revitalize your early childhood program. Trying to create sustainable changes to a program's quality without a vision is as ineffective as expecting your GPS device to lead you on a journey before you have programmed where you want to go.

Ways to Build Momentum

Having a clear vision can thrust you into the energizing cycle of an upward spiral in your program. However, committing to bringing your vision to life is professionally challenging for some leaders. It is essential to see beyond the barriers and envision your program fully living your vision.

I am deeply inspired by the Reggio Emilia approach to education, which originated in Reggio Emilia, Italy, after World War II. The school and community leaders' commitment to intentionally and continually improving their programs has helped Reggio schools achieve recognition as some of the best preschools in the world. Steve Seidel, a researcher at the Harvard Graduate School of Education, states, "It seems always better to be on a difficult—even extremely difficult—path than a path that, in my heart, I believe won't lead where I want to go. The challenge and beauty of coming to know the experience in Reggio is to confront the possibility that I could work—as they have—with others to create the reality I would like to live in . . . whatever the demands of that creative act."

Starting this vision-focused journey will definitely place some new demands on school leaders. The beauty of this work, whatever the short-term stress of moving toward a new system of leadership, is that you will be able to create a new strengths-based reality for your program to thrive in. Early childhood leaders need to become inspired to move their programs from stale complacency into vibrant, thriving learning environments. The lasting benefits from this shift will be felt in every facet of the program. Teachers, administrators, parents, and—most important—children will reap the benefits of being part of a flourishing community.

Steps for Creating a Shared Vision

If you want to increase the passion, intentionality, and engagement of every member of your learning community, you need to create a shared vision that becomes the driving force that guides and inspires everyone's actions and interactions. Creating a collaborative vision statement is a process that requires focus, planning, and open communication. The strategies and activities laid out in this book are designed to guide you as you cocreate a vision statement and then bring it to life in your learning community. Here is an overview of this empowering process:

1. Clarify the focus. What are the key areas you would like to focus on to enhance the quality of your program? What is the positive impact you want to make in the lives of children, teachers, and families?

2. Use reflective practices to identify the core values of your program. This book contains examples such as creating vision boards.

3. Select a series of reflective exercises to work through as a group to identify the core values of your program. Clarifying these values provides the foundation for writing a vision statement that honors and strengthens the long-standing ideals of the program.

4. Use appreciative inquiry to tap into all that is possible. Facilitate meaningful discussions around these questions: If you had three wishes to transform this program, what would they be? If we could look into a crystal ball and see this program operating at its very best, what would we see? What would you be doing? What would the children be doing? What would be the most exciting thing you would notice?

5. Synthesize all your reflections—key words, themes, and messages. Create word lists and summary statements that reflect all the key messages gathered from your reflective activities and appreciative inquiry exercises.

6. Write a draft. Form a committee, selecting staff members that reflect the diversity of your program. Be sure to include new and longtime staff and a mix of teachers and administrators. Some programs involve members of their boards and parent representatives. Work together to review your notes and keyword lists from all the activities. Then create two or three draft vision statements to share with the entire staff. Strive to create drafts that are clear, compelling, empowering, and motivational.

Linking Your Vision to a Program Administrators' Assessment Tool

Vision statements are used as an indicator of quality in the early childhood field. The Program Administration Scale (PAS) is a tool developed to accurately measure the leadership practices of early childhood programs. In the PAS documentation, Teri Talan and Paula Jorde Bloom define a vision as "a statement of an ideal that can be used to motivate, inspire, and guide the center toward a desired future state." Mission statements clarify an organization's purpose and its current status; they are useful for strategic decision making.

In the strategic planning section of the scale, a program's vision and mission statements are rated using the following criteria:

- *Inadequate*—The center does not have a written mission or vision statement.

- *Minimal*—The center has a written mission or vision statement.

- *Good*—Staff members and the center's governing or advisory board were involved in developing or reviewing the written mission or vision statement.

- *Excellent*—The center's mission or vision statement is reviewed at least every five years by staff members and the center's governing or advisory board.

7. Gather your community to work on revising and redrafting. Choose a time to reflect on the vision statements. Discuss wording preferences, likes, and dislikes. Also, find ways for people to give candid and confidential feedback—distribute note cards at the meeting or have them complete a short survey, either on paper or online.

8. Share your vision. Make the vision statement visible in all aspects of the program. Create visually appealing posters with the vision statement and place them in the entranceway, classrooms, and teacher spaces. Select photos that capture the essence of the vision statement and create a photo board display of the vision in action. Change the photos frequently to keep the board appealing and interesting. Use the vision statement on your website, in newsletters, blogs, job postings, and marketing materials. Read the vision statement at parent nights, staff meetings, and board meetings.

9. Live the vision. Create the momentum needed for the vision to come to life by finding ways to incorporate the vision's key message in your daily work with children, teachers, and families. Use the vision as the foundation for creating meaningful and relevant professional development goals and learning experiences for teachers, administrators, and the program. Successfully weaving the vision into the daily life of the program will build a renewed sense of purpose, will increase engagement, and will, with persistence, lead the program to new levels of quality.

Moving Forward with Confidence

To successfully create the program transformation detailed in your vision statement, you as a leader must have full confidence in your ability to make it happen. As inspirational coach Jack Canfield says, "Whether you call it self-esteem, self-confidence, or self-assurance, it is a deep-seated belief that you have what it takes; the abilities, inner resources, talents and skills to create your desired results." You need to step into your role as a director with full confidence in your own competence. This will create the positive energy to inspire everyone in your program to fully engage in their work and the work of transformation. Fully committing to using your vision statement as a guiding light will allow you to keep your attention focused on where you want to go, rather than on what is stopping you. It will support you in leading with confidence.

# Align!

Following NAEYC's Strategic Planning Guidance

The National Association for the Education of Young Children (NAEYC) advises that an early childhood program should have a strategic planning process that outlines actions for accomplishing the following:

- Implementing the program's vision and mission

- Achieving outcomes desired for children

- Maintaining high-quality services to children and families

- Providing long-term resources to sustain the operation of the program

A strategic plan is intended to ensure that programs conduct self-evaluations and reflect on their current practices to improve services provided, and then make a plan for how to implement those improvements. The following examples can serve as evidence to document these accomplishments:

- Plans for professional development

- A formal statement of a program's quality goals

- Informal or formal reports on how the program is carrying out its mission

- Surveys that are distributed to families and used to inform strategic planning

Sample Vision Statements

Vision statements can be short or long. The key is that they capture the essence of where you want your program to go. Creating a vision statement involves opportunities for rich, meaningful dialogue among all those involved in the program. In the exercises section at the end of this chapter, you will find a variety of strategies for generating the dialogues necessary to write a vision statement that is truly reflective of the aspirations of all those involved in your program. The examples here show what is possible.

EARLY CHILDHOOD COOPERATIVE

"Our vision is to create a nurturing environment rich in respect, individuality, and support for diversity. We acknowledge people's strengths and challenges and encourage everyone to try new skills regardless of the outcome. We allow for individuality and growth by focusing on positive contribution and consistently using clear, honest communication."

LARGE COMMUNITY-BASED PROGRAM

"Our vision is to create a thriving early education and child care program that deeply respects and nurtures the potential that exists in each child, teacher, and family. Through ongoing collaboration and open communication we will establish a vibrant community where joy, learning, creativity, and meaningful relationships flourish."

PRESCHOOL PROGRAM

"Our Vision for Sunny Brook . . .
Is to be a place where the
ORDINARY can become the EXTRAORDINARY.
Where we start each day anew and Open-minded
so we can see and believe the Endless Possibilities
and Uniqueness in our Sunny Brook Community!
Recognizing Children as individuals . . .
we will bring out their strengths by
Listening and being Flexible to their ideas and needs.
We will be Respectful and Inclusive of all Families.
As a Staff . . . we will remain Positive and Work Together.
We will stay Confident in who we are;
Encouraging each other to reach our Full Potential."

LARGE PUBLIC-SCHOOL PROGRAM

"We will live the dream to work together and respect each other, which will create a fun, developmentally appropriate environment for ALL to flourish. By using research-based practices through play and creative learning experiences, the HPS Early Childhood Program provides a strong foundation for learning and actively engaging families and the community where all members are key players in a positive learning environment."

SMALL COMMUNITY-BASED PROGRAM

"At the PATCH Early Childhood Center we embrace the joy, energy, sense of wonder, and inner beauty of each child, teacher, and parent. We create vibrant and peaceful classroom environments where children are free to explore and the teachers are intentional about creating child-centered learning opportunities. We value the cultures of the children and families to foster their growth and independence. We are committed to providing nurturing early learning experiences that form the foundation for the children's educational journeys!"

AFTERSCHOOL PROGRAM

"To create an environment where children, teachers and parents are respected, valued, and fully engaged in all aspects of our program."

Reflective Practice Exercises

Creating a vision statement that is truly collaborative and reflective of all the constituents of your program is a multistep process. The following exercise will generate the key insights into the core beliefs and program aspirations that are the essential ingredients for a vibrant, collaborative vision statement. Doing each exercise is not necessary. Select the ones that are most relevant to you and gather the rich data that each exercise produces to write your vision statement.

BIG ROCKS DEMONSTRATION

In order to develop a vision statement that is grounded by the core beliefs of your organization you need to spend some time identifying your guiding principles, or in leadership guru Stephen R. Covey's phrase, *big rocks*. Why do you exist? Who do you serve? How do you serve them? What are the reasons you do what you do every day? Once these foundational principles are named, you can begin to move forward. This exercise helps the group to clearly define guiding principles—big rocks that shape and define the program.

Materials needed: Chart paper and marker, a quart Mason jar, 10 to 12 rocks (golf ball size or a bit larger), a bag of smaller rocks (large pebble size), and a bag of tiny rocks (fish tank stones work well).

Process:

1. Take the glass jar and place it on a table in front of the group. Then simply say, "This glass jar represents your professional life here at Caring for All" (substitute your program's name).

2. Ask participants what core values shape their work. Prompt them with follow-up questions: What brings you the greatest joy? Why do you work here? What gets you out of bed and into the program every day? When friends ask why you work here, how do you answer them? The

answers to these questions will generate the big rocks. For each response, put a big rock in the jar, and use chart paper to record the big rocks of the program.

3. Ask the group what day-to-day tasks fill up the jar of their professional life. The group will have a large number of responses (paperwork, planning, meetings, and so on). For each response, throw in a small handful of the medium-size rocks.

4. When the jar is almost full, ask the participants what small tasks of their professional lives fill up their jars. I often refer to this as the minutia of our daily work. Participants will have many responses, such as wiping noses, changing diapers, and cleaning. For each response, throw in a small handful of the tiny rocks.

5. When the jar is full to almost overflowing, stop and hold the jar up. Remind the group that the jar represents their professional life, and ask the pivotal question: What would happen if the big rocks were not placed in the jar first? The response is clear and always includes "They wouldn't be in there" or "They wouldn't fit," and similar statements. One of my favorite responses was "They would be buried out in the playground."

6. Debrief the key message from the exercise: We need to keep the big rocks—the reasons for doing the important work we do with children, families, and each other—at the center of all we do.

You can end this exercise here, and you will have an invaluable list of the big rocks for your program. However, completing the next steps takes this exercise to a more vibrant conclusion and gives you the opportunity to add new big rocks to your list.

Extended Activities

Classroom- and administrative-team reflections: Divide the group by classroom teams, and, if possible, have an administrative team. Ask participants to work in their groups to discuss and define their own big rocks for their work together in the classrooms. If you like, give the groups a reflection sheet containing the following questions:

- What are your big rocks for your team? What do you care most about? What are your top priorities?

- Are you willing to make a commitment, right now, to put those big rocks in the glass jar of your life?

- What steps will you take to be sure the big rocks get in your jar of life first?

The sheet gives them a way to focus their conversation. When you collect the sheets after the exercise you'll have more big rocks to add to the initial list.

Classroom- and administrative-team skits: This step produces amazingly positive energy and brings a sense of true ownership to the big rocks of the program. Ask each team to develop a list of big-rock rules that will help them remember to put their big rocks in first. Then ask each team to create a short skit, poem, story, word play, or rap to perform for the whole group that reflects their big-rock rules. Encourage the groups to use any props that might be available in the program. Have a camera on hand to take pictures and videos of these powerful performances. When I share this idea with directors, many tell me that their staff members will never be willing to carry out the performance. Guess what? They all do! Seeing each other's skits is inspiring to the whole staff.

Debrief the skits: Be sure to have a follow-up discussion. Ask what participants learned about their big rocks. Do you have more big rocks to add to the initial list? What are the most important things you can do to keep the big rocks in the jar of your professional life?

Hopes and Dreams

This activity is, by far, one of the simplest ways to learn your parents' and teachers' aspirations for the future of your program.

Materials needed: Index cards and pens. When doing this exercise with different groups, such as parents and teachers, I use different colors of index cards for the groups (parents, teachers, administrators, or board members).

Process:

1. Set the stage. Discuss with the group that you would like to get shared perspectives on their hopes and dreams for the program. This exercise can be broad or specific. For a broad perspective on overall expectations for your program, ask for their hopes and dreams for their program in the next year or two years. For parents, it is important not to go too far into the future, as their child will age out of the program. For teachers, administrators, and board members, you can extend the timeline. Examples for a specific focus include the learning environment and social interactions.

2. Distribute index cards. Ask participants to write their hopes and dreams on index cards, one idea or thought per card.

3. Collect the cards.

4. Read the statements back to the group. People are often reluctant to share and read their own cards, so create opportunities for all the cards to be read without having individuals read their own. You can ask for volunteers to come up and read the cards back to the group with you. Or distribute the cards back to the group and ask everyone to read one. Again, ensure that participants do not read their own cards. One of the most powerful experiences I have had with this exercise was to do this first with teachers and then with parents at a parents' night event. After

I collected the cards I distributed them back to the parents in the room and then gave each teacher a card to read (not their own). Then, round-robin style, parents and teachers stood up and read the cards back. The sense of unity among the eighty people in the room was palpable. I can still recall the energy that created a driving force for our program that year.

5. Debrief. After all the cards have been read, ask the group: "What are the common themes? How do the hopes and dreams relate to the continued growth of the program?" Collect all the discussion points on chart paper.

6. Create a hopes and dreams list. Type up all thoughts on the index cards and the notes from the debriefing. Share them with participants and use them as guide points for creating your vision statement.

Optional Follow-Up Activities

After doing this exercise at a parents' night, I thought we should somehow tie the hopes and dreams into our end-of-the-year family event. I decided to create a video containing photos from the school year and quotes from the hopes and dreams cards. It showed the parents that we honored their thoughts and brought them to life daily in the program. The result was a moving and inspirational evening that allowed parents to see firsthand how valuable their thoughts were in shaping all aspects of our program.

CHAPTER 2

Infusing the Learning Community with Positive Energy

Positivity can uniquely revitalize your worldview, your mental energy, your relationships, and your potential.

—Barbara Frederickson, *Positivity*

Positive energy is vital to creating and sustaining strengths-based learning communities that allow children and teachers to thrive. The research is clear on the importance and impact that a positive environment has on building strong relationships and attaining positive learning outcomes. Leaders need to be constantly tuned in to the social and emotional environments of their schools, as well as throughout every classroom and across all relationships. It is essential that school leaders and teachers understand that the culture and climate they create in their classroom are some of the most important aspects of their work.

Research on Leadership and Quality Learning Environments

A study published in 2007 in the *Journal of Research in Childhood Education* by Joanna K. Lower and Deborah J. Cassidy reports that the quality of early childhood programs is related to the leadership practices of the administrators there. Using data from three early childhood assessment tools—the Program Administration Scale (PAS), the Early Childhood Work Environment Survey (ECWES), and the Early Childhood Environment Rating Scale—Revised (ECERS-R)—the researchers observe that "a relationship between child care quality and child care work environments, including program administration and organizational climate, is supported. This study supports the idea that child care leadership and management practices and organizational climate are correlated with global quality."

The deep importance of creating positive environments is further supported by the research findings on toxic stress and brain development being conducted at the Center for the Developing Child at Harvard University. Their research findings, noted in *The Science of Early Childhood Development*, stress that "the essence of quality in early childhood services is embodied in the expertise and skills of the staff and in their capacity to build positive relationships with young children." Leaders' responsibilities in relation to the culture and climate of their programs are also highlighted in the National Association for the Education of Young Children (NAEYC) Accreditation Standard 10.A.07. "The program administrator and other program leaders systematically support an organizational climate that fosters trust, collaboration, and inclusion." The guidance for that standard notes, "The program leaders have systems, plans, policies, or procedures in place that are inclusive of all staff, show support for staff, build mutual trust, and foster support and collaboration between staff."

The early childhood field is facing major challenges in creating learning environments that foster the healthy growth and development of young children. The energy in early childhood programs can vary and shift from year to year, classroom to classroom, and even day to day. Being a climate engineer is a vital role for leaders of early childhood programs. As a leader, your top priorities are to stay present and aware of the emotional environment and provide strong leadership through support and resources when energy is fluctuating. Sometimes, the energy levels drop slowly. Without any support or resources, before long a program that was once full of joy and positivity can find itself drowning in negativity.

The signs of negativity in an early childhood program may seem subtle at first but become increasingly more visible when you know what to look for. Leaders need to watch for the following indicators that their school environment is becoming toxic:

- Gossip
- Staff complaints, criticism, or distrust of leadership
- Staff use of negative language to describe children or their parents
- Negative subgroups within the staff
- Lack of focus on the positive things happening in the program

Recognizing the signs of negativity early and addressing them with staff members can prevent negativity from becoming rampant throughout the program.

A Journey Down the Negative Spiral

One program director, Judy, reached out to me at a time when the energy of her program had sunk to an all-time low. After many years of leading a highly regarded program, Judy was faced with the realization that the culture and climate of her program was full of negativity. When I asked her to describe what was happening, she had a hard time pinpointing exactly what had shifted. Judy decided it would be beneficial for her staff members to send me anonymous notes describing the challenges they were facing. The following excerpts from these powerful notes clearly highlight that the culture and climate of the program had become dangerously unstable:

- "In the last few years, we have lost our sense of a school community."
- "We need to reestablish a sense of trust and respect for each other."
- "The school is very polarized. There was a time when our strength was our sense of collaboration."
- "We need to stop alienating colleagues."
- "We are skilled at working with children to teach them respect and cooperation. Why are we not modeling this in our adult relationships?"
- "Do we have a clear mission? How do we define who we are and the work we do? What are our core values?"
- "We need to stop the backbiting and gossip that is rampant in our program."
- "We need to find ways to improve communication between staff members and to have more effective staff meetings."

Although Judy was shaken and emotional when I shared the extent of the concerns the staff expressed, she admitted that she was not surprised. After processing this information, Judy felt relieved that she had clarity of the situation and was ready to move forward to do whatever was necessary to stabilize and reenergize the program.

This program is not alone in the challenges it faced. Many programs go through downward energy spirals. It is important to recognize when negative energy is seeping into programs and to find ways to build supportive, collaborative, strengths-based environments that can quickly rebound from these periods of low energy.

Understanding the Power of Positivity

A first step in moving a program from the overwhelming impact of negativity is to fully understand how a positive approach can transform programs. Judy's story is not unique. Early childhood leaders have struggled with managing gossip, negativity, low levels of engagement, and stressful classroom environments for far too long. With the new research correlating healthy childhood development with positive, engaging environments for young children, the time has come to facilitate a dramatic shift in the overall climates of early childhood programs.

In order to reverse the effects of negative energy, we first need to fully grasp the broad and lasting impact of positivity. Barbara Fredrickson, a researcher and a widely recognized expert on the connection between positive emotions and leadership, provides many valuable insights for early childhood leaders who are intent on enhancing the organizational climate of their programs. In her book, *Positivity,* she identifies ten forms of positivity—joy, gratitude, serenity, interest, hope, pride, amusement, inspiration, awe, and love—that are all integral aspects of daily experiences with young children. The more we open ourselves up to seeing and experiencing positivity, the greater the benefit to our overall health, as well as the well-being of each individual and the learning community as a whole. The vibrant energy created through an ongoing focus on what is going well is key to revitalizing relationships and increasing engagement in our schools.

When we share positive emotions, we can bring out the best in individuals. Finding new and meaningful ways to shine light on the strengths of each individual will have a dramatic impact on overall energy and the learning community. While I was coaching a director who was working hard to bring more positivity into her work with her teachers, she shared this inspiring feedback with me: "Thought you'd enjoy knowing that after nine years of being a director I finally had a staff member sit down and tell me, 'I always look forward to reading my final evaluation. It always picks me up and reinforces that I am doing things right!'" The small changes that this director was making were creating ripples of positive energy throughout her program.

On the other end of the spectrum, negativity has a way of subtly seeping into school communities. Positive interactions can change the flow of negativity. Shifting conversations from the downward spiral of negativity takes practice, but with persistence, positive dialogue can successfully act as a reset button to the damaging impact of negative conversations. Every day in every interaction, we have the opportunity to subtly or significantly increase the positivity that we are bringing to the conversation. If you recognize that every small change can have a considerable impact, you can fuel your journey to creating a flourishing learning community.

Positivity ignites the upward spiral within each of us and allows us to see all that is possible. What is truly remarkable is that positive energy is contagious. As your positivity increases, you spark a more positive attitude in everyone around you. The generative nature of the upward spiral can create lasting change in the culture and climate of schools.

Fredrickson powerfully states the value of positivity and its impact on key facets of our schools—joy, creativity, and play. Negative emotions can narrow a person's perspective on options available, but positive emotions can broaden our view of possible actions. "Joy, for instance, sparks the urge to play and be creative," Fredrickson notes. "Interest sparks the urge to explore and learn, whereas serenity sparks the urge to savor our current circumstances and integrate them into a new view of ourselves and the world around us."

These comments inspire further thinking on the role of joy and creativity in our schools. Carlina Rinaldi, president of the education organization Reggio Children, clearly states the importance of creativity in the adults who educate children. "We should remember that there is no creativity in the child if there is no creativity in the adult: the competent and creative child exists if there is a competent and creative adult," she notes in *The Hundred Languages of Children*. Because it is abundantly clear that one of the most important goals of early childhood education is to holistically foster the creativity and competence of children, we need to find new ways to nurture and grow environments where positivity is an essential value of all programs.

Strategies for Transforming a Program's Energy

Creating an energy shift in your program often feels like a monumental task, but it is doable. Focus on highlighting the existing assets of the program while incorporating new strengths-based strategies. This will create the momentum you need to move from a negative climate to a positive one.

SELF-ASSESS YOUR LEVEL OF POSITIVITY

The Positive Energy Wheel graphic will help you determine how positivity is showing up in your professional work with teachers, children, families, and colleagues. Take a minute to reflect on the past week and then circle the number in each section that represents the degree of each form of positivity you are experiencing. The higher the number, the more you are experiencing each form of positivity.

By completing the wheel, you will have a new perspective on how positivity is showing up in your professional life and the areas you would like to enhance. Use the results of this exercise to find ways to increase positivity in new and energizing ways. Increasing amusement and joy in my program was something I practiced daily. I still smile when I think of the times I was able to transform the energy of my work environment by simply having fun. My favorite antics included climbing to the top of the jungle gym and telling the children I couldn't get down, wearing my favorite Goofy hat to a staff meeting, reading Robert Munsch books to the children, or just joining the children in their play. Create a list of ways you can increase positive energy in your program, and then encourage your staff to complete the Positive Energy Wheel exercise and develop lists for their classrooms.

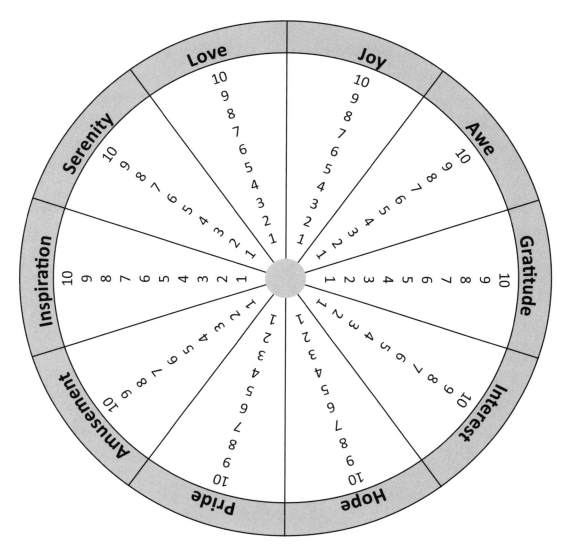

Positive Energy Wheel

ENGAGE IN APPRECIATIVE INQUIRY

Appreciative inquiry focuses on acknowledging and validating the existing strengths of the program and every individual in the school community. This approach is based on the *heliotropic principle*, which states that plants grow toward the light. This simple biological principle is at play in all of our interactions and relationships; figuratively, we all feel the pull of the light. By finding new ways to shine light on the strengths of our learning community, we will create renewed energy for growth and change.

This strengths-based approach to change helps everyone to feel valued for their contributions and excited to use their strengths to support the whole community. Each and every day, seek ways to illuminate the strengths of your program and each person in it. Becoming intentional about observing strengths can take practice. Start by finding moments throughout the day to quietly observe teacher and child interactions. Share what you notice with the teachers, either in person or in a handwritten note. Gather your positive reflections and weave them into individual, team, and schoolwide meetings to create the energy necessary to move out of the downward spiral and into a community where positive transformation can occur. Make your positive observations visible by writing about them in your newsletter, in a blog, or on your website. Shifting our daily dialogue is a critical first step in improving the overall climate of a program. Find new ways to have reflective individual and group conversations that focus on these key questions:

- What's the best thing that is happening in our program right now?
- What do you value most about working here?
- What is your vision for the ongoing success of this program?
- How does working here inspire you to give your best?
- What do you value most about how we work as a collaborative team?
- If we were to be given an award as one of the top early childhood programs in the country, what would it be for? How did we work together to achieve this honor?

Add a sense of magic and fun to your conversations with these questions:

If you had a magic wand and could transform any aspect of your teaching, what would you change? How would this one change improve the quality of your teaching? How would it benefit the children in your classroom? What would be the lasting impact of this change?

The answers to these questions will help you to shine the light on what is right in your program. They will support you as you develop new strengths-based approaches and transform the culture and climate of the learning community.

The five principles of appreciative inquiry shown in the graphic work together to support what all school leaders are hoping to achieve—positive outcomes. The pyramid illustration shows how positive attention, anticipation, questions, interactions, and energy can build on each other to form the strong foundation for strength-based actions and outcomes to occur.

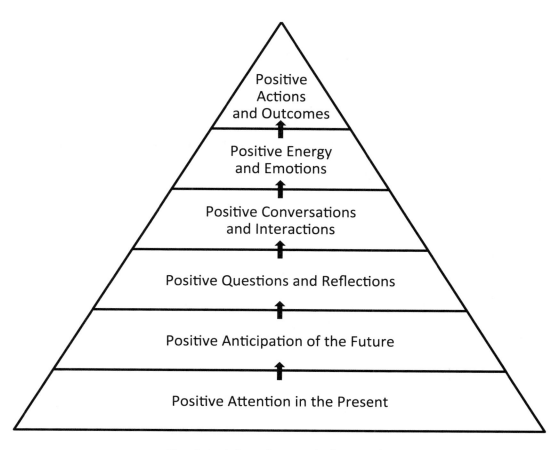

Five Principles of Appreciative Inquiry

Source: Adapted from *Evocative Coaching: Transforming Schools One Conversation at a Time* by Bob Tschannen-Moran and Megan Tschannen-Moran. ©2010 Jossey-Bass. Reprinted with permission.

INVITE EVERYONE ABOARD

Positive transformation will not occur unless all members of the learning community are engaged and willing to move forward with the necessary changes. The negative energy of one individual in an organization is powerful enough to put the brakes on any efforts to improve the program.

In *The Energy Bus*, Jon Gordon provides guidance on how to overcome negativity and create passion-driven teams whose work is fueled by positive energy. As a school leader, you must wholeheartedly embrace your role as the driver of the program's bus to bring lasting, systemic change to the culture and climate of the program. Fully realizing that a leader's actions—and, in many cases, lack of action—contribute to a program's negative climate is an essential premise of Gordon's ten rules for promoting a great ride:

- As the program leader, you're the driver of the bus.
- Desire, vision, and focus move the bus forward.

- Positive energy fuels the trip.

- Invite people along for the ride, sharing your vision for your course and destination.

- Don't waste energy on people who will not come aboard.

- Don't give space to passengers who will drain the energy of others aboard the bus.

- Recognize that shared enthusiasm attracts more travelers and keeps them aboard.

- Express appreciation for your passengers.

- Drive with a destination in mind.

- Enjoy the shared trip.

For more in-depth exploration of Gordon's guidance, visit the Energy Bus website (http://www.theenergybus.com/).

Creating Environments That Reflect Joy and Wonder

The energy of an early childhood program is palpable from the moment we pass through the doorway. Energy is evident in every nook and cranny of the program, whether the program is in a bright, shiny new building or, as often is the case, in the basement of a building that was never designed to house an early childhood program. Some of the most vibrant and joyful programs are operating in less-than-desirable buildings.

Every school leader has the opportunity to positively affect the environment of the program. In the book *Inspired and Unstoppable*, Tama Kieves encourages us to "Keep cooking up the magic even if you're in the corner of someone's basement. Magic is magic. Where there's energy, there's something alive."

Creating environments that reflect and celebrate the joy, magic, and beauty of daily life in an early childhood program is not always easy. In a 1991 article in *Child Care Information Exchange*, Reggio Emilia advocate Lella Gandini states: "One of the greatest challenges in designing institutions is to transform a physical plant into a human environment. One part of this transformation has to do with discovering ways to make impersonal rooms and hallways reflect the lives of children and adults who spend so many active hours in that space." The best way to do that is to think more deeply about the people in your program. Think about what their lives are like, what their past experiences have been, what motivates them, and what they can contribute from their family culture. You should also consider the history of your school and what the organizational culture has been like. Take a careful look at every aspect of your physical space. It's the first step in making environmental changes that reflect the vibrant lives of the children, families, and teachers who participate in your program.

Everyone can play a role in promoting more positive energy in the school environment. Such teamwork helps to build communication and facilitates necessary program changes. The following ideas and strategies will help you begin this process:

- Invite teachers, parents, and children to share photographs, collections, and special treasures. Create beautiful displays throughout the program that showcase the interests and passions of all members of the community. Place engaging and visually appealing biographical boards of teachers and staff throughout the building. Change these displays throughout the year.

- Ask teachers to stand in the center of their classrooms and take photographs of all four corners of the room. Have them bring the photos to a staff meeting, and facilitate a discussion around what they noticed. Ask them to share ideas for changing their environments to more fully reflect the beauty of the relationships and learning that is happening there. Repeat this exercise throughout the year to keep environments energized and refreshed.

- Encourage teachers to visit other schools with the specific focus of observing the environments. Share new ideas and inspirations at a staff meeting.

- Find inspiration in unique places—children's museums, furniture stores, and home design catalogs.

- Invite teachers to create a private page or interest board on social media so they can collect and share ideas to enhance the environment.

- Solicit ideas for environmental changes from families.

- Set aside a small portion of your supply budget to allow teachers to buy a unique item that reflects a core value of their classroom.

- Share images of inspiring environments at a staff meeting, and talk about what new ideas teachers are excited to bring into their classrooms.

- Create a scavenger hunt that challenges teachers to go through the building looking for evidence of how the environment reflects the lives, interests, and joyous moments of everyone in the school. Have them share what they found that inspires and excites them. Develop a list of what they feel is missing and new ideas for making what is missing visible.

- Investigate new ways to create documentation that reflects the vision and values of the program. What are the key messages of the documentation in the classrooms, entranceways, and hallways? Do they align with your core values and beliefs? Develop a list of ideas for changes and enhancements.

- Encourage small changes. These small changes will promote the energy and momentum needed to create an environment that shines a light on all the beauty and wonder that exists in your program.

Gathering Data

To facilitate positive growth, leaders need to have a clear picture of where the energy of their program is. Often, however, there is a large gap between how the director and the teachers perceive the organizational climate. Data is extremely useful in helping leaders understand the impact of their leadership style. In the book *The 5 Languages of Appreciation in the Workplace: Empowering Organizations by Encouraging People*, Gary Chapman and Paul White point to decades of research showing that employees' perceptions of organizational climate are based primarily on the manager's style of leadership and behavior.

One way to gather information about perceptions is to survey your teachers and staff. Results from a confidential survey can strengthen the early childhood program by guiding leaders to implement changes that are fully aligned with the needs and desires of their staff. Building trust and collaboration is the key to long-lasting, sustainable improvements in program quality.

Data also can provide the strong beacon of light needed to guide a program out of the stormy seas of disequilibrium that negative energy can create. After hearing a vivid description of the negative climate a large community-based program was engulfed in, I suggested that the leadership team gather current, accurate data that would help them understand the issues they were facing. After reviewing some survey options, they decided to have the entire staff complete the Early Childhood Work Environment Survey through the McCormick Center for Early Childhood Leadership. The results were eye opening to the leadership team. The responses unearthed a wide range of issues related to trust, collegiality, and supervisor support. The staff included detailed comments in their survey responses that helped the administrators gain clarity on the depth of the issues. The following comments are reflective of the nature and tone of many responses:

- "Coworkers have toxic relationships with each other. Many gossip about other coworkers' personal and professional business."
- "People say pretty bad things about each other off the record."

- "Most teaching staff is very upset with administration for one reason or another."
- "Some staff are favored over others: staff are overly scrutinized in their practice and criticized unfairly for their interactions with parents and coworkers."

Although in some ways the data was surprising and unsettling, it was essential information for the leadership team to acknowledge and process. The results from the survey were shared with the staff members and provided motivation to move out of the negative spiral they had been swirling in for far too long. Staff members felt that their issues were heard, and they were able to collaboratively develop a comprehensive professional plan. Team members were willing to fully engage with the plan to create positive, lasting changes in their program.

Organizational climate can be assessed in a variety of different ways. Distributing a survey to the whole staff is a valuable first step in obtaining a broad perspective on how everyone in the organization feels about the culture and climate of the program. The Early Childhood Work Environment Survey (short form) is an easily administered tool that provides clarity on a staff's perceptions of the organizational climate of the program.

This survey was developed by Paula Jorde Bloom and is available in *Blueprint for Action: Leading Your Team in Continuous Quality Improvement*. Additional resources for gathering data to better understand the work environment include the following:

- The Early Childhood Work Environment Survey (http://newhorizonsbooks.net)
- NAEYC Self-Assessment Teaching Staff Survey (http://naeyc.org/)
- "My Director" survey in *Leadership in Action: How Effective Directors Get Things Done* by Paula Jorde Bloom
- Classroom Assessment and Scoring System (CLASS) (http://www.teachstone.org/)
- Program Administration Scale (PAS) (http://mccormickcenter.nl.edu/)

Align!

Understanding the Dimensions of Organizational Climate

The dimensions of climate identified by Paula Jorde Bloom and described below provide a powerful lens for looking at how teachers perceive the environment they work in.

Ten Dimensions of Organizational Climate

Dimension	Definition
Collegiality	The extent to which staff are friendly, supportive, and trusting of one another. The peer cohesion and esprit de corps of the group.
Professional growth	The degree of emphasis placed on staff's professional growth. The availability of opportunities to increase professional competence.
Supervisor support	The degree of facilitative leadership providing encouragement, support, and clear expectations.
Clarity	The extent to which policies, procedures, and responsibilities are clearly defined and communicated.
Reward system	The degree of fairness and equity in the distribution of pay, fringe benefits, and opportunities for advancement.
Decision making	The degree of autonomy given to staff and the extent to which they are involved in centerwide decisions.
Goal consensus	The extent to which staff agree on the philosophy, goals, and educational objectives of the center.
Task orientation	The emphasis placed on organizational effectiveness and efficiency, including productive meetings, program outcomes, and accountability.
Physical setting	The extent to which the spatial arrangement of the center helps or hinders staff in carrying out their responsibilities. The availability of supplies and materials.
Innovativeness	The extent to which the center adapts to change and encourages staff to find creative ways to solve problems.

Source: Bloom, Paula Jorde. 2015. *Blueprint for Action: Leading Your Team in Continuous Quality Improvement,* 3rd ed. Lake Forest, IL: New Horizons. Reprinted with permission.

A multitude of forces can affect the energy of school environments, and identifying those forces is essential to creating a more dynamic school community. When you increase positive energy in your center, you will see rewards in every facet of the program. As a leader, it is up to you to step forward and inspire your staff to work together in creating the changes necessary for your program to thrive.

Reflective Practice Exercises

Increasing positive energy in early childhood programs requires a willingness to dive into deep, meaningful conversations that will help to define the key attributes of the learning community teachers want to create. Open communication is fundamental to the process of building a positive environment.

As you work to facilitate reflective conversations, consider the following reflective pieces and questions as ways to bring new, provocative, and engaging discussions to staff meetings. As a leader, it is key that you select reflections that are relevant and meaningful to you. Use the ones listed here or search for quotes, poems, or articles that resonate with you to generate meaningful discussions about the culture and climate of your program.

DISCUSSING WAYS TO HONOR CHILDREN

Canadian songwriter and performer Raffi Cavoukian has written "A Covenant for Honouring Children," which can serve as a starting point for a discussion about how your program views children.

> We find these joys to be self-evident: That all children are created whole, endowed with innate intelligence, with dignity and wonder, worthy of respect. The embodiment of life, liberty, and happiness, children are original blessings, here to learn their own song. Every girl and boy is entitled to love, to dream, and to belong to a loving "village." And to pursue a life of purpose.

> We affirm our duty to nourish and nurture the young, to honour their caring ideals as the heart of being human. To recognize the early years as the foundation of life, and to cherish the contribution of young children to human evolution.

> We commit ourselves to peaceful ways and vow to keep from harm or neglect these, our most vulnerable citizens. As guardians of their prosperity, we honour the bountiful Earth whose diversity sustains us. Thus, we pledge our love for generations to come.

Raffi, the founder of the Centre for Child Honouring, has made the covenant available for download on his website (http://www.childhonouring.org/covenantprinciples.html), and you can also watch a

YouTube video clip of the covenant before having small groups discuss it (https://www.youtube.com /watch?v=Mp61lUu8VaA).

Once you have shared the covenant with your staff, ask them to discuss the following reflective questions in small groups:

- What message is Raffi giving us about the essential characteristics of environments where young children can thrive?

- How is our program creating a loving village? Provide some examples. What can we do to strengthen the loving village?

- What peaceful ways are we committed to? Share ideas for bringing more peace into our daily work.

CONSIDERING WORDS THAT JOIN OR DIVIDE

Read the poem "Clothesline" by Marilyn Maciel and discuss it in small groups:

"Clothesline"

> *i*
> *you*
> *us*
> *them*
> *those people*
> *wouldn't it be lovely*
> *if one could*
> *live*
> *in a constant state*
> *of we?*
> *some of the most*
> *commonplace*
> *words*
> *can be some of the biggest*
> *dividers*
> *they*
> *what if there was*
> *no they?*

what if there

was only

us?

if words could be seen

as they floated out

of our mouths

would we feel no

shame

as they passed beyond

our lips?

if we were to string

our words

on a communal clothesline

would we feel proud

as our thoughts

flapped in the

breeze?

Ask staff members to reflect on the poem and discuss the following questions in small groups:

- What messages are you receiving from the poem?

- What does the poem say about the importance of a positive, strengths-based work environment?

- How does this poem make you think differently about the impact of communication in your program?

THINKING ABOUT WORDS AS WEAPONS

The following proverb is attributed to Native Americans from the Hopi tribe, but the source is unconfirmed. Still, you and your staff can learn from the message:

Take care

when you speak in judgment.

Words are powerful weapons

which can cause many tragedies.

Never make a person look like a fool with your tongue.

Never make a person look small with your big mouth.

A hard word, a sharp word,

can burn a long time,

deep in the heart,

leaving a scar.

Accept that others

think differently,

act differently,

feel differently,

speak differently.

Be mild and healing with your words.

Words should be light!

Words should be calm.

Bring people together,

Bring peace.

Where words are weapons,

people face each other

like enemies.

Life is too short and our world is much too tiny

to turn it into a battlefield.

Ask staff members to reflect on this passage and discuss the following questions in small groups:

- What key message does this passage communicate to you?

- How does this passage relate to positive relationships with your coworkers? With parents? With children?

- If you could take two or three lines from this passage and post them in your classroom, which lines would you choose?

- Share key points of your discussion with the large group.

Creating Vision Boards

It is important that teachers become fully engaged in creating a shared vision for the future of the program. You can do this by creating vision boards during a staff meeting, or by asking the staff to come to the staff meeting with vision boards they have already created.

Ask staff members to imagine that it is a particular year in the future and your program is now vibrant, energized, and an amazing place for children and teachers to live and learn together.

Provide the following instructions:

- Using an 8-by-10-inch piece of paper, illustrate exactly what is happening in your vision.

- You can use magazine cutouts, words, cartoons, drawings, or photographs to illustrate your vision.

- Your vision boards will form the foundation of our work together at our next staff meeting.

At the next meeting, divide the staff into groups of four or five, and have them do the following:

- Share their vision boards.

- Summarize the key points of the group's visions on chart paper.

- Share their key points with the larger group.

After the meeting, type up a summary of the key points from all the groups, and develop a plan to begin to bring their visions to life.

Engaging in an Appreciative Inquiry Exercise

The following activity gives staff the opportunity to engage in rich, focused discussions around positive work environments. This exercise is best done in a four-hour time block. If you need to do this in shorter segments, you can complete the first two focus activities during session one and the remaining two focus areas during the next session.

Focus Session 1: Your Best Experience in a Vibrant Learning Community

Provide participants with the following instructions.

1. Select a partner from your school whom you know the least about.

2. Recall one of your best experiences in a vibrant learning community you have been part of.

3. Describe it to your partner, including the following elements in your story:

   - What was happening?

   - Who was involved?

   - How did you participate?

   - In what ways was it energizing, engaging, and valuable to you?

   - What did you value most about yourself in the situation?

   - What was beneficial about the intention and nature of the community and its work?

   - How well was the activity organized?

Focus Session 2: Sharing Stories of Vibrant Learning Communities

Ask the interview pairs from the first focus session to combine and form groups of four or six and follow these instructions:

1. In your small groups, interviewers can introduce their paired partners and share highlights of their partners' stories of vibrant learning communities.

2. As you listen respectfully, focus on the common themes that come up in the stories.

3. Designate someone in your small group to record members' comments on chart paper.

4. Think about all the stories you've heard, and share what you think are the best or most successful attributes of vibrant learning communities. These form the positive core—those factors that make it vibrant, energizing, and satisfying.

5. Select a story that you all agree reflects most of the common themes.

6. Discuss what you would choose if you had three wishes for increasing the positive energy in your early childhood community, and record those wishes on chart paper.

7. Appoint a member to share your group's discussion items with the other groups. Each group will share the story that reflects the common themes of the group, their list of positive core attributes, and their three wishes for a flourishing community.

Focus Session 3: Future Possibility—Collective Dream

Ask participants to work in the same groups as the previous focus session, and follow these instructions:

1. You fall into a deep sleep and wake up refreshed. It's one year later, and you are an active and engaged member of your early childhood program. Now the program is operating at its best. Think about these questions:

   • What is going on that engages you fully?

   • What is contributing to its success?

   • How are you incorporating your strengths—your positive core—and your three wishes?

2. In as creative a way as possible, describe, illustrate, draw, or perform a skit, a rap, or a song that captures the essence of your vibrant early childhood community.

3. When you are ready, each group will share the members' collective dream!

Focus Session 4: Codesign Your Community

Ask participants to work in the same groups as the previous session and follow these instructions:

1. As you think and talk about your dream for a vibrant learning community, what are the key design elements you will include from your dream that will give greater vitality and energy to it? For example:

   • What are the activities?

   • What is your stated purpose?

   • What are your articulated values?

2. Designate someone to record ideas on chart paper, and then create a list of the key design elements that are discussed.

3. Ask group members to vote in some way (possibly by sticking dots on the chart paper) for which areas they would like to focus on.

4. Pick spots in the room for different groups to meet and discuss the top choices.

5. Select one of the design elements that you know something about or one that you are very interested in knowing more about. Meet with other participants in the room who are interested in the same element. Together, you can decide how this element will help your community flourish.

6. In your new group, create a compelling future possibility statement of how your element will add life, vitality, and energy to your community.

7. Ask a group member to share your compelling future possibility statement with the whole group.

Source: This activity was adapted with permission from Robyn Stratton-Berkessel's "Flourishing Communities Worksheet" in the book *Appreciative Inquiry for Collaborative Solutions: 21 Strength-Based Workshops* (pages 110-111). San Francisco: Pfeiffer.

CHAPTER 3

Developing Purposeful Professional Development Plans

Young children are best able to become lifelong learners when they spend their days with teachers who are devoted to lifelong learning on their part.

—Valeri R. Helterbran and Beatrice S. Fennimore, "Collaborative Early Childhood Professional Development: Building from a Base of Teacher Investigation"

The importance of effective, engaged, and educated early childhood teachers is clear, as research continues to show how important preschool learning is for later school success. With only 2,000 days between birth and kindergarten, all children deserve to spend their days in high-quality programs with educators who are continually enhancing their skills to best meet the needs of every child in their care.

Energizing early childhood teachers to stay passionate and excited about their own professional development is an ongoing challenge for school leaders. Complacency and stagnation can become the norm, unless leaders are consistently focused on the essential role of supporting the professional growth of teachers. To create sustainable growth, leaders need to be skilled in helping to craft professional development plans through an interactive process that builds on the teachers' strengths, interests, and passions. When completed through a collaborative process, such plans create detailed and well-defined road maps to guide beneficial growth and change.

Strengthening the systems that increase the effectiveness of early childhood programs has long-lasting implications for children's academic and social competence and therefore for society.

The Cascading Effect

When children experience high-quality education in the early years, the positive effects can last a lifetime, according to Alvin Tarlov, a physician, educator, and researcher. The benefits to children in high-quality programs when compared with those who do not have these opportunities tend to include the following:

- Improved readiness for kindergarten

- Successful start in school

- Fewer behavioral problems

- Rewarding interpersonal relationships

- Effective learning

- Less tobacco and drug use

- Decreased delinquency and truancy

- Fewer juvenile justice encounters

- Higher graduation rates

- Higher college entrance and completion rates

- Higher inventory and better flexibility of job skills

- Better jobs

- Stronger and more stable family life

- Higher income

- More upward social mobility

- Greater engagement in community

- Better health and well-being

The Value of Individual Professional Development Plans

Focusing on a holistic approach while crafting an individual professional development plan (IPDP) is the key to developing effective plans. The early childhood field employs assistant teachers, teachers, support staff, and administrators who vary widely in their own educational backgrounds, ethnicities, cultural and linguistic characteristics, and skills and abilities. Working collaboratively with each individual can strengthen professional relationships and ensure that IPDPs meet and respect educators' diverse needs.

Ideally, professional development plans will be living documents that guide school leaders to become fully engaged not only in the individual teacher's professional growth, but also in the growth of the program. IPDPs and program development plans serve three primary functions:

- A guide for the future professional development of the teacher or administrator

- A tool to guide career development

- A plan that lays out the appropriate pathways and specific action steps needed to achieve the goals

Research on the importance of IPDPs has shown a positive impact. Teacher educator Nancy Sugarman points to a Kentucky study's findings that "teachers who developed and used IPDPs were more likely to have consistent quality in their classroom environments, to remain in the field of early care and education, and to pursue their educational goals." In addition, Sugarman noted in an article in *Young Children*, these factors tended to lead to better outcomes for the children. As researchers learn more about the brain development of children, the expectations for the knowledge and skills that a preschool teacher needs to improve education outcomes are rapidly increasing. Encouraging teachers to embrace their own professional development is essential for keeping pace with these changes.

School leaders are often frustrated at the lack of professional growth that they see in their teachers from year to year. In many programs, leaders hold some type of annual meeting with teachers to write goals for the upcoming year. Once the goals are agreed on, the teachers and administrator sign the required form. Unfortunately, in far too many cases the process ends there. This flawed approach has led to a lack of engagement and focus on achieving the goals. Year after year, the cycle continues because teachers encounter a void of energy, support, and guidance. If leaders will take the time to rethink their actions, they can find ways to stop the merry-go-round of setting the same goals without achieving results. Bringing the goals into an integrated system that guides, supports, and facilitates their achievement is the key to sustainable quality improvements.

Align!

Linking Individual Professional Development Plans to NAEYC Standards

NAEYC standards 10.E.10 and 10.E.11 advise educators to craft IPDPs at least annually during the staff evaluation process, and revisit them in between as needed. Beyond writing the IPDP, program leaders should have an implementation strategy. Goals should include providing clear orientations for new staff, offering credit-bearing work to existing staff, and improving credentials and competencies.

In terms of the program's professional development plan, standard 10.E.12 advises basing the overall plan on needs identified through staff evaluation and a program evaluation process. The written program plan should include mentoring and coaching, discussions of ethical issues, and training in the program's policies and procedures.

A System for Supporting Professional Growth

Using an intentional system to support teachers can reduce stress, increase engagement, and lead to higher quality teaching and improved learning outcomes. The requirements for teacher development have been increasing as states have adopted higher standards for early childhood teachers through their QRIS. I have developed an integrated system designed to help leaders align the many tasks of supervisory support and leadership. This system incorporates the key supervisor functions found in QRIS models and links to NAEYC accreditation requirements.

This model provides leaders with a system for integrating the many aspects of their supervisory responsibilities to support teachers in moving forward and achieving their professional goals. For many school leaders, the fundamental tasks of supporting teachers' development are already part of the work they do. However, these tasks—writing goals, conducting observations, providing feedback, reviewing data, and planning professional development—in and of themselves do not enhance the professional growth of teachers. When these tasks are done in a fragmented way, their effectiveness is limited. It follows, then, that creating a system that aligns these supervisory tasks is key to increasing the positive results of these actions. If you examine the graphic showing the elements that make up this system, you will notice that the components build from the bottom up and encircle each other in support, surrounded by the vision.

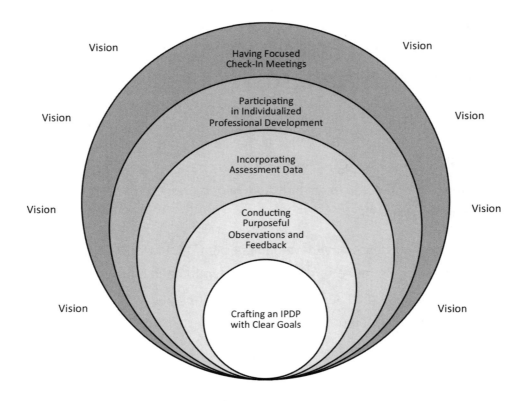

A System for Supporting Professional Growth

VISION

Vision is the supporting framework for this model. Clearly defining the vision of the individual or program is essential to building engagement with the professional development plan. Sharing stories of professional hopes and desires is important to creating a meaningful vision. When goals are strongly connected to the vision, the energy to achieve the goals increases. Review chapter 1 for resources on creating a vision.

IPDP WITH CLEAR GOALS

Goals are the core of every professional development plan, and they should be crafted to reflect the vision of the individual or program.

Goals should reflect professional needs, strengths, and current performance and should include pertinent information from assessment data. The more relevant the goals, the greater the focus will be on achieving them. Leaders who wish to empower teachers and staff will invite them to cocreate goals. The intent is to increase educators' engagement in their own professional growth and the commitment of everyone involved.

Linking the goals to the state's early learning standards builds a connection to quality and helps educators grow and develop in all competency areas. Goals are most easily achieved when they include a specific timeline for completion and detailed action steps. To increase accountability, consider the attributes of SMART goals:

> S—specific
>
> M—measurable
>
> A—attainable
>
> R—relevant
>
> T—time-bound

Other tips for writing goals include using action verbs (such as "I will *communicate . . .*" or "I will *strengthen . . .*") and outlining precise details. Regardless of the goal, keep in mind that progress will be more noticeable—and teachers will feel more encouraged—if larger goals are broken into smaller ones.

Purposeful Observation and Feedback

Goals can provide the lens through which colleagues conduct meaningful observations. Review the goals often and schedule observations that will provide insight into the degree of progress. To make observations effective, follow them up with concrete feedback and discussions.

Incorporating Assessment Data

Data from program evaluations, parent evaluations, and assessment tools can provide valuable insights and benchmarks. Data can open our eyes to see what is truly happening versus what we think is happening. Leaders need to review all data that has a link to the teachers' performance and use that information when facilitating the goal-setting process. When the goals are linked to data it becomes possible to use ongoing data to inform the progress being made to achieve the goal.

Individualized Professional Development

Selecting relevant professional development opportunities directly linked to the teachers' goals can play a pivotal role in supporting growth. Strategic leaders target funds, time, and energy toward goal achievement. Other important considerations are the learning styles and preferences of each teacher. Incorporating a variety of professional growth opportunities—coaching, mentoring, workshops, conferences, visits to other schools, and courses—will support increased learning and retention of knowledge.

In many instances, professional development for individuals and programs has been selected based on interests instead of goal-related needs. Develop a master list of the goals for the program, for each teacher, and for each administrator to guide them in planning and budgeting for professional development activities offered to individual staff members and the program as a whole.

Focused Check-In Meetings

Throughout the year, hold reflective meetings focused on assessing the progress of the professional development plan. A minimum of three check-in meetings per year is a good target. At these meetings, you can acknowledge the growth that has been achieved and strategize how to support continued goal achievement.

Case Studies Showing the System in Action

When this system is brought to life, intentionality and focus increase for the leaders and the teachers. The best way to illustrate this system is through detailed examples.

A Teacher's Professional Development Journey

Lisa was an experienced teacher in the three-year-old classroom at our center, and her professional development needs were not initially clear to me. She had completed her bachelor's degree, demonstrated strong curriculum skills, engaged well with parents and coteachers, and created a beautiful learning environment.

Crafting a Teacher IPDP

I used an intentional process to collaborate with Lisa to discover her professional development needs and to create a meaningful IPDP. At the start, to fully understand Lisa's vision for her own professional growth I needed to provide her with an opportunity to reflect and then to share her thoughts with me. I scheduled an individual meeting with her and sent her a reflection sheet to complete in advance. The reflection sheet, which would guide our discussion, contained the following questions:

- What has been the highlight of your work as a teacher this year?
- What is the biggest challenge you are facing in your daily work as a teacher?
- What are your hopes and dreams for your professional life in the next three years?
- How can I best support you in overcoming your challenges and reaching your goals?

When Lisa came to the meeting, her sheet was full of notes, and she was hesitant at first to discuss her responses to the questions. But once she did, I knew that Lisa trusted me to share not just her joyous moments but also her biggest challenges.

After telling a rich story that highlighted the importance of building a relationship with a hard-to-reach parent, Lisa shared a challenge that she had not previously been able to express. She talked about wanting to be able to manage her emotions and reactions when children pushed her buttons. It was a real surprise to me that this was Lisa's challenge. She always appeared calm and dealt with challenging children in appropriate ways. When I shared my thoughts about her skills in this area, she acknowledged that she felt she did have some strengths. Lisa explained that although she had many classroom management skills, she did not always use her skills in the same way with every child. She wanted to find resources and support that would help her stay calm and use her skills consistently with all children. Lisa was very clear how this short-term goal related to her long-term vision. She wanted to be able to overcome this challenge so she could more confidently move toward her dream of being a professional trainer and mentor to new teachers in the field.

At the end of our initial meeting I asked Lisa to take all that we talked about and draft a couple of goals for herself. I informed her that I would use our notes to also draft some goals. We met the next week to share our goals, and they were very much in sync. Together we refined the wording and agreed on the following goals for Lisa:

- Short-term—I will monitor and record my own emotional reactions to children and their behaviors to better understand what pushes my buttons.
- Short-term—I will develop new strategies to respond to all children and all challenging behaviors effectively and consistently.
- Long-term—I will begin using my skills to support, mentor, or train early childhood teachers.

Once the goals were established, we worked together to develop an action plan for each goal, as noted in the table that follows.

Lisa's IPDP Sample Action Plan

Goal 1. I will monitor and record my emotional reactions to children and their behaviors to better understand what pushes my buttons.

Action Steps	Resources Needed	Timeline	Links to Standards	Status
a. Use a notebook to track reactions. Record specific situation, child, and reaction. b. Review notebook weekly to see what patterns emerge. c. Discuss observations with supervisor. d. Clearly identify the situations, behaviors, and children that push my buttons.	Notebook schedule of biweekly meetings with supervisor	Begin recording reactions and behaviors on Oct. 1. Schedule bi-weekly check-ins with supervisor Oct. 15 through Dec. 15.	Massachusetts Core Competency 2: Guiding and Interacting with Youth	

Goal 2. I will develop new strategies to respond to all children and all challenging behaviors effectively and consistently.

Action Steps	Resources Needed	Timeline	Links to Standards	Status
a. Find and attend a course or workshop on challenging behaviors. b. Read a book or three articles related to understanding why children push the buttons of adults. c. Meet with supervisor to outline new strategies I will be using to effectively manage challenging behaviors.	Listings of available workshops and courses Suggested reading list of books and articles	Attend workshop or course before Dec. 15. Complete readings by Dec. 15.	Massachusetts Core Competency 2: Guiding and Interacting with Youth	

(continued on next page)

Lisa's IPDP Sample Action Plan (continued)

Goal 3. To begin using my skills to support, mentor, or train early childhood teachers.

Action Steps	Resources Needed	Timeline	Links to Standards	Status
a. Brainstorm a list of the ways my skills could benefit other early childhood teachers. b. Discuss my list with my supervisor to find a way to use my skills to create a mentor relationship with a new teacher in the program. c. Find and complete a course (approved for CEU or credit) that will support me in developing, mentoring, or training skills. d. Join a local early childhood professional association (a local chapter of NAEYC) and participate in meetings and workshops related to professional development. e. With the support of my supervisor, create one workshop that I could present at a staff meeting. f. Revise workshop presentation and create a workshop proposal to send to local training agencies.	A listing of local early childhood associations Fees for joining an early childhood association Listing of local professional development courses Listing of funding opportunities for courses Sample workshop planning templates Sample workshop proposals Listing of local early childhood training agencies	Develop list by Nov. 1. Set up a mentor relationship beginning Jan. 1. Join an early childhood association by Jan. 1. Create workshop for staff meeting by March 1. Send workshop proposal out by April 30. Complete a course in mentoring or training by June 30.	Massachusetts Core Competency 8: Professionalism and Leadership	

The format for developing IPDPs can vary according to each state's requirements. Check with your local licensing organization or the agency that supports your QRIS to see if you need to use a specific format. A listing of each state's QRIS office can be found on the website for the QRIS National Learning Network (http://www.qrisnetwork.org).

Conducting Observations and Feedback

Lisa's IPDP provided a new lens for me to observe her in the classroom. Knowing that she wanted to learn more about her own reactions to challenging behavior, I looked for opportunities to observe her during high-stress moments of the day. I asked Lisa to give me some examples of when she felt most stressed by challenging behavior and when she felt children were pushing her buttons. Her responses included "the time between the end of rest time and afternoon play," "when I am bringing the children in from the playground," "settling specific children into rest time," and "when children are restless at circle time." Simply asking Lisa this question helped me to step away from my standard observation times and schedule myself in the classroom at times that would provide the most useful feedback to Lisa.

After each observation, I scheduled time for a feedback session that focused on an interactive dialogue with Lisa. In formulating these highly focused strength-based discussions, I followed the Harvard Project Zero see-think-wonder routine: What did I see? What did I think? What did I wonder? These conversations, combined with Lisa's reflection from her own journal of her reactions to challenging moments, helped us unearth key issues and patterns. Raising Lisa's awareness was the first step forward in supporting her ability to make changes.

Incorporating Assessment Data

Lisa needed to see the broad picture of her strengths as a teacher and identify areas of growth so I could help her to develop and achieve her goals. I felt the issue of managing her reactions and emotions was only one facet of who Lisa was as a teacher. I wanted her to be secure in her strengths, so she would have the energy necessary to make the changes she desired. Reviewing the data that I had available from parent feedback surveys, Teaching Strategies Gold reports on the skill development of the children in her class, and ECERS helped me to highlight her many skills as a teacher. In a film called *Celebrate What's Right with the World,* Dewitt Jones captures the importance of this step: "By celebrating what is right, we find the energy to fix what is wrong." Using data to shine the light on educators' strong points creates the momentum for them to appreciate their strengths and continually grow as professionals.

To gain clarity and a big-picture understanding of how Lisa's internal reactions might be affecting the classroom environment, I brought in a consultant to do an assessment using the Classroom

Assessment Scoring System (CLASS). The consultant explained to both of us that the CLASS focuses on effective teacher-child interactions as a key measure of classroom quality. The CLASS also provides a common language for discussing effective teaching. In addition, this tool helps answer questions about the range of experiences children have when interacting with their teachers, the relation between teacher-child interactions and children's learning and development, and changes in the effectiveness of classroom interactions in response to different professional development opportunities.

The data from this assessment gave Lisa a deeper understanding of the key areas that she could improve on. After the initial assessment, Lisa was excited to move forward and implement new strategies to better meet the needs of the children in her classroom. She was eager to have the assessment done again after six months to be able to see the progress she was making.

Participating in Individualized Professional Development

The specificity of Lisa's goals helped shape the professional development activities she would participate in. Together we researched courses and reading material. Lisa was thrilled when she found a two-part course specifically focused on how teachers can better interact with the children who push their buttons. The course was an hour's drive away and spread out over three evenings. When I told Lisa we could likely find something closer, she said, "No, this is the one." Her commitment to expand her knowledge and move to a new level of professionalism was rewarded. After the first session, she reported that this course was exactly what she needed. She gained insights into her own emotions and behaviors and began thinking about new strategies to use in the classroom. Lisa also found a course approved for CEUs that was focused on designing and delivering workshops. The course helped to open her eyes to all the ways she could use her skills to create an effective and inspiring workshop for teachers.

Knowing that many staff members shared the goal of managing their responses to challenging behaviors, I decided to use some of our programwide professional development time and money to hold a workshop for the entire staff that focused on dealing with children who push your buttons. After seeing how useful the CLASS assessment and data were for Lisa, I offered a full staff training on CLASS. This staff training provided the impetus for the teachers to honestly discuss this sensitive topic openly and to develop some peer mentoring opportunities. Creating experiences for the whole staff to grow and develop in this area provided lasting benefits to the program.

Focused Check-In Meetings

Finding time to meet with staff individually is often a huge challenge for school leaders. Not finding the time is the biggest barrier to supporting the ongoing growth and development of teachers. In

Lisa's case, we were able to combine some of her biweekly check-ins regarding her reflection journal with feedback from the observation sessions. This reduced the number of sessions but kept the dialogue flowing and our attention focused on achieving the goals. Three times during the school year we went over the IPDP form to fill in the status column. These check-in meetings were short, but they were the key to Lisa achieving her goals. Creating the time to build a shared commitment to the achievement of goals facilitates professional growth in profound ways.

Align!

Using Reflective Questions to Develop Meaningful Goals

The following types of questions can be adapted and customized to meet the needs of each individual educator.

Questions for recognizing and engaging the teacher's strengths:

- What is the best experience you have had as a teacher? How can you replicate this experience in the coming year?

- What skills are supporting you in your daily work as a teacher?

- What do you consider to be the three best things that are happening in your classroom right now?

- If one year from now we were meeting to discuss the high level of success you experienced as a teacher, what would be the focus of our conversation?

- Describe what you love and enjoy most about your role as a teacher.

- Share an example of what helps you to do your best work as a teacher.

- What are your future dreams and aspirations? What is the one thing that most excites you about your future?

- What has been the most effective professional development experience you have had in the last two years? How did this experience affect your work as a teacher?

(continued)

Questions for envisioning and defining areas of growth:

- If you had three wishes to bring new energy, focus, and purpose to your work, what would they be?

- What new skills would you like to develop to enhance your effectiveness in the classroom?

- What support or resources can I or other colleagues provide to support you in doing your best work?

- In what ways could I support you in achieving new levels of success in your role as a teacher?

- What new credentials would you like to add to your professional portfolio in the next two years? Five years? Why are these credentials important to you as a teacher?

Create a reflection sheet for educators using two or three questions from each category. Keep the questions fresh and inviting by changing them up each time you meet. This will help you have engaging conversations that tap into the passions of each educator.

An Administrator's Professional Development Journey

Overseeing and supporting early childhood programs requires increasingly complex knowledge and skills. It is crucial that leaders continually assess their own professional development needs. Often leaders are so busy taking care of the business side of the program and the ever-present needs of children, teachers, and parents that they do not take the time to focus on their own areas of growth. Donna was one of those leaders when I began working with her. Using the same system that supported Lisa, Donna worked on her professional growth with her supervisor.

Crafting an IPDP for an Administrator

Donna felt her work as a school leader had become stagnant. She was spending far too much time at her desk dealing with demands from her board, new licensing requirements, and her state's quality initiatives. As a requirement of a leadership course I was teaching, Donna needed to reflect on her own vision for her professional growth and develop an IPDP to guide her out of the rut she was stuck in. She crafted the following vision statement:

My work with teachers will be engaging and intentional. The work that teachers do brings me great joy. I want this joy to spill over to them and into their classrooms through their teaching and nurturance of young children. My hope is that our assessment system will become richer and more authentic through meaningful and focused observations and collections of children's learning and that our new curriculum will continue to inspire teaching and lead towards more Project Approach experiences in classrooms.

I want to build on family engagement through more intentional home/school connections and bring families in closer connection to their children's learning experiences.

I envision all of my classrooms as places of joy, where teachers and families work together in providing the children with all that they need. Whenever anyone enters any of the classrooms, I want them to instantly feel vitality, energy, and love of learning.

Donna was able to write an inspirational vision statement that deeply connected to her heartfelt desire to enhance her own leadership to better the lives of the teachers, families, and children she directly influenced. The next step for Donna was to lay out a detailed plan that would bring the vision to life.

Donna's IPDP Sample Action Plan

Goal 1. Authentic assessment				
Action Steps	**Resources Needed**	**Timeline**	**Links to Standards**	**Status**
a. I will receive training in Teaching Strategies Gold (TSG) to better support teachers in effectively using this assessment tool. b. I will develop a planning tool that will help teachers organize a system for observing, recording, and connecting observations to the needs of each child. c. I will develop a resource guide for teachers on how data collection is enhanced by adding photos to children's portfolios. d. Through individual meetings, team supervision meetings, and monitoring, I will guide teachers through this process and support their progress.	Listing of available TSG training sessions Sample planning forms and digital cameras A binder for each classroom for storage and organization of materials	Receive training by Sept. 30. Develop planning tool by Nov. 1; present at the all-staff meeting on Nov. 11. Develop resource guide by Nov. 1; distribute at the all-staff meeting on Nov. 11. Provide guidance through monthly meetings.	Massachusetts Core Competency 6: Observation, Assessment, and Documentation	

(continued on next page)

Donna's IPDP Sample Action Plan (continued)

Goal 2. Curriculum support				
Action Steps	**Resources Needed**	**Timeline**	**Links to Standards**	**Status**
a. I will schedule time away from the office—to visit at least one classroom a day to interact with the staff and children. This will refresh my mind and incorporate my love for teaching. b. I will gather data from teachers on what topics/themes really interest the children. I will find new ways to support curriculum questions, and the sharing of ideas and encourage deeper discussions at team and full-staff meetings. c. I will support staff in raising CLASS scores above the national average by May 1. CLASS observations will occur at the beginning and middle of the school year, in order for me to see and compare strengths and needs to further plan professional development and training. This will happen through CLASS videos, observations, and feedback through supervision. d. I will work closely with our mentor coach on addressing the ideas, thoughts, and expectations from our teachers on what worked, what did not, and what needs more.	Find new online scheduling tool to use to create a visual schedule A firm contract with a CLASS mentor coach for observations and training Purchase CLASS videos and reference books	Schedule time away immediately. Beginning in September, do monthly check-in with teaching teams. Ongoing data gathering with monthly check-ins with each classroom team. First CLASS observation by Oct. 1. Monthly check-in meetings with mentor coach.	Massachusetts Core Competency 5: Learning Environments and Curriculum	

(continued on next page)

Inspiring Early Childhood Leadership

Donna's IPDP Sample Action Plan (continued)

Goal 3. Professional growth				
Action Steps	**Resources Needed**	**Timeline**	**Links to Standards**	**Status**
a. I will sign up for an eight-session director's educational group this fall. This will give me a professional break once a month to stretch my mind and grow my leadership skills while also interacting with other professionals in my educational field. b. I will enroll in an online strengths-based coaching course. This will strengthen my ability to interact with staff and families in a reflective, understanding manner.	Enrollment forms for director's leadership group and funding approval Enrollment forms and funding approval Purchase required book	Director's sessions once a month, September to May. Weekly coaching course sessions for thirteen weeks, beginning Sept. 30.	Massachusetts Core Competency 8: Professionalism and Leadership	

Goal 4. Family engagement				
Action Steps	**Resources Needed**	**Timeline**	**Links to Standards**	**Status**
a. I will increase family engagement and find one new way each month to help families connect to the work that is happening in the classrooms. b. I will complete the strengthening families training to develop new strategies for supporting the many needs of the families in our program.	A monthly calendar that highlights family events in each classroom Enrollment information for strengthening families training	Monthly ideas beginning Sept. 1. Complete training by Nov. 1.	Massachusetts Core Competency 3: Partnering with Families and Community	

The format for developing IPDPs can vary according to each state's requirements. Check with your local licensing organization or the agency that supports your QRIS to see if you need to use a specific format.

Conducting Observations and Feedback

One of the biggest challenges for school leaders is having a system of accountability linked to their IPDP. Often, school leaders receive minimal supervision and support from the individuals in leadership positions above them. Some leaders, especially owner-operators of programs, do not have anyone to consistently guide their professional development efforts.

Donna was fortunate to have an off-site supervisor who worked collaboratively with her to finalize the IPDP. Together they built time into their monthly supervisory meetings to check in on the progress of the goals. This format for developing a vision statement, IPDP goals, and action plans, which was required for the course, was a new experience for Donna and her supervisor. By working together they were able to strengthen their professional relationship and build a system of accountability that helped Donna achieve her goals.

Self-accountability is an essential component for staying focused on the IPDP. One way to enhance accountability is for leaders to share their goals and action steps with all relevant constituents—teachers, board members, parents, and supervisors, if they have one. Another option is to build accountability through a coaching relationship. Many states have coaches available through their QRIS funding. If formal coaching is not an option, finding a colleague through a local leadership group and scheduling monthly check-ins focused on the IPDP will help to keep leaders focused and moving toward achieving their goals. Donna's accountability was enhanced by the strong supportive relationships that she developed in her monthly leadership group. Donna also tapped into the wisdom and knowledge of the state-funded CLASS coach for guidance in achieving her goals related to classroom interactions.

Incorporating Assessment Data

Building assessment data into the IPDP helps to create specific benchmarks for achievement. Donna included raising scores from the CLASS assessment in one of her goals. Seeing progress, however incremental, in these scores over the course of the year helped Donna support the changes she was striving to create.

Donna also used the Strengthening Families Self-Assessment Tool for Center-Based Early Care and Education Programs to gather data on how her program was supporting the families. She put together an in-house team to complete this assessment to be sure that the perspectives of teachers, parents, and board members were reflected. Once the self-assessment was completed, the team prepared a summary report highlighting areas where the program was most successful in supporting families and areas that the program needed to enhance. Together the team prioritized action steps that would guide Donna in achieving her goal of increasing family engagement throughout her program.

Obtaining relevant feedback from teachers and parents regarding leadership goals is another essential element for guiding growth. Combining the use of feedback from evaluation and assessment tool forms with specific questions related to the IPDP goals can provide meaningful and relevant feedback. Donna created her own online survey to get feedback from her staff on how to support their curriculum and assessment needs. Using the Survey Monkey (https://www.surveymonkey.com/) online resource, Donna gathered data that gave her a deeper understanding of the issues her staff were facing and helped her create new ways of working with teachers that directly addressed their needs.

Participating in Individualized Professional Development

Leaders are often faced with the challenge of finding relevant, inspirational, and results-oriented professional development opportunities. The IPDP can create the clarity needed for leaders to step out of the box and find new professional development opportunities that will help them succeed.

As Donna developed her vision and goals, she could see where she needed to focus her professional development. She knew that she needed to be up to speed on the curriculum and assessment tools (CLASS, Teaching Strategies Gold, and Strengthening Families) required by the quality initiatives linked to her funding sources. These tools were new to her program, and her teachers had received some training related to the tools through state-funded programs. However, Donna had only a fundamental understanding of the tools. Increasing her competence in these areas helped her support the teachers with a new level of confidence.

Donna also realized that ongoing connection with other school leaders would help break down the isolation she felt being the sole administrator in her building. Attending the monthly leadership group and actively participating in the online coaching program fueled her energy and her desire to stay out of the rut she had been stuck in.

Having Focused Check-In Meetings

Donna's plan had built-in checkpoints that helped her stay on track. She created an online calendar with specific colors for her leadership activities, and scheduled progress checks so she didn't lose track of her goals. By checking in on a consistent basis with her teachers, a mentor coach, a colleague from her leadership group, and her supervisor, Donna was able to stay focused and move past the inevitable obstacles that come up during periods of growth and change.

The Impact of Integrated Professional Development Plans

These two examples illustrate how an integrated system can support the professional development of teachers and administrators and positively affect program quality and child outcomes. Teachers and administrators can benefit from the plans by collaboratively defining clear goals and expectations; supervising with intentionality and positive energy; creating accountability check-ins; and consistently following through. While creating plans for professional growth, educators may find it helpful to place those goals in the context of career achievements they envision for themselves. The activity that follows encourages teachers and administrators to stretch their perspectives further into the future.

Reflective Practice Exercise

WRITE YOUR RETIREMENT SPEECH

Whether you are retiring in the next five years or not for 25 years, it is important to reflect on this key question: "What will people remember me for?" Think about your core values, professional goals, hopes, and dreams. Then take a blank piece of paper and vividly describe the following:

- The accomplishments that you are most proud of

- Your greatest professional achievement

- The key people who influenced your work

- The leadership values and principles that guide your work

Be as descriptive as possible, using the words in the list that follows to spark ideas. Once you have written your retirement speech, use it as inspiration to make the changes necessary to bring all that you desire to life!

The ABCs of Strengths-Based Leadership

Acceptance	Communicative	Empathetic
Accommodating	Community builder	Empowering
Accountable	Competent	Encouraging
Appreciative	Confident	Energetic
Approachable	Considerate	Engaged
Authentic	Courageous	Equitable
Autonomous	Creative	Ethical
Aware	Credible	Facilitative
Benevolent	Curious	Fair
Brave	Decisive	Fearless
Calm	Dedicated	Flexible
Candid	Delegator	Focused
Clear	Dependable	Forward-thinking
Climate engineer	Determined	Genuine
Collaborative	Dynamic	Goal-oriented

Gracious	Nonjudgmental	Role model
Happy	Objective	Self-aware
Helpful	Observant	Skilled
Honest	Open	Strategic
Humble	Optimistic	Supportive
Inclusive	Organized	Team-focused
Innovative	Original	Thought-provoking
Inspiring	Passionate	Timely
Instinctive	Pleasant	Transformational
Intelligent	Positive	Transparent
Intentional	Present	Trustworthy
Interactive	Proactive	Unwavering
Intuitive	Proud	Upbeat
Joyous	Quality-conscious	Validating
Kind	Quick	Vigilant
Knowledgeable	Receptive	Virtuous
Listener	Reflective	Visionary
Loyal	Resourceful	Warm
Mindful	Respectful	Welcoming
Moral	Responsible	Well-informed
Motivational	Responsive	Wise
Nice	Results oriented	Zealous

CHAPTER 4

Engaging in Continuous Quality Improvement

We need to be able to stand before these children in 20 years and say, "I did my best by you." In 30 years, we need to be able to say, "The world is in good hands because I valued you enough to provide you with a quality education, and you are now able to lead the next generation."

—Brenda Powers,
Boston Association for the Education of Young Children

For quality improvements to truly take hold, leaders need to fully commit to assessing the strengths and areas of growth for all aspects of their program and then consistently take the steps necessary to facilitate the changes. Linda K. Smith, deputy assistant secretary for Early Childhood Development at the Administration for Children and Families, U.S. Department of Health and Human Services, states: "Continuous quality improvement is about creating an environment where management and workers strive to create constantly improving quality. It's a process to ensure that programs are systematically and intentionally improving services and increasing positive outcomes for the children/families they serve."

Her words—*systematically* and *intentionally*—speak to the heart of the challenges faced by early childhood leaders. Naturally, educators want to be connected to high-quality programs. Yet many leaders feel adrift in the sea of changes as they try to navigate through the many local, state, and national quality initiatives. School leaders are often overwhelmed by time constraints, staffing issues, and all the juggling of priorities required to manage their programs successfully. Being intentional about quality improvement requires leaders to look at their programs through a broader lens.

Almost every state is developing and using a QRIS to provide a framework for continuous quality improvement. The systems vary in different states, but they all are designed to improve the quality of early childhood programs and outcomes for children and families. When leaders engage with the QRIS in their state, they are working with a well-researched and standards-based framework for incrementally increasing the quality of their program.

A QRIS can be a guiding light as educators embark on the journey to move their program up the quality continuum. Leaders who model a positive attitude and communicate the importance of the standards, assessment tools, and programmatic requirements provide support for their staff to move past their fear of change. No QRIS is perfect, and many leaders may be challenged by a standard or requirement that does not make sense to them. Leaders can find a way to advocate for adjustments in the system, while not allowing an area of disagreement to create a negative attitude toward the overall QRIS. If staff members sense negativity coming from the school leader, a culture of fear and resistance can quickly develop and block any attempts at change. Therefore, fully involving staff in rich dialogues and reflective activities that shape the change process is essential.

Developing a Program Improvement Plan

A well-developed program improvement plan provides leaders with a process that promotes ongoing quality improvement. Measurable goals and realistic timelines for completion will hold leaders and staff accountable for achieving the desired outcomes.

The following tips and strategies will guide you through the development of a program improvement plan:

- Never lose sight of why you are working toward improving quality. Remind yourself and the staff that creating the highest quality program you can for the children and families you serve is at the heart of why you exist as a program.

- Involve the staff in each step of the process so that the plan is meaningful and relevant to them.

- Remember to consistently honor the strengths of the program and use those strengths to facilitate and support the achievement of the goals outlined in the plan.

- Review all sources of data from surveys, assessments, and IPDPs to gather evidence on the program's areas of strength and potential growth.

- Fully commit to staying intentionally focused on the plan.

Align!

Linking Program Plans to NAEYC Standards

When creating a professional development plan for your program, refer to the relevant NAEYC standards to make sure you are on track.

10. E. 11

The program has an implementation plan for professional development, including orientations for new staff. Credit-bearing course work is included in the professional development plan whenever possible. The plan improves staff credentials and competencies. It is updated at least annually or as needed based on the evaluation process, the need to keep staff's knowledge current, or other identified needs.

10. E. 12

The program's professional development plan:

- is based on needs identified through staff evaluation and from other information from program evaluation process
- is written and shared with staff
- includes mentoring, coaching, and other professional development opportunities for staff
- includes discussions of ethical issues
- includes training in the policies and procedures of the program

---

- Allocate the time and financial resources needed to complete the initial plan and achieve the goals and action steps.
- Keep staff updated on progress at staff meetings and through your newsletters. Celebrating progress will create the momentum needed to keep moving forward.
- Use the improvement plan as a reference point when you are developing IPDPs for yourself as the program leader, as well as for all administrators and teachers.
- Use classroom observation time to identify progress on the goals and action steps.
- Provide consistent concrete feedback to teachers to support their ongoing professional growth.

- Invite parents to be active participants in the process. Consider inviting them to join a committee, complete surveys related to the program improvement, participate in work days to enhance the environment, or raise funds to support specific goals. Use their skills and expertise to help achieve your goals.

- Keep parents, board members, and other partners informed about the steps you are taking to improve program quality.

- Make progress visible—document achievement of specific goals with photos, videos, and written anecdotes. Focusing on progress, however small, will maintain everyone's energy as you keep moving forward.

- Meet regularly with teaching teams, supervisory staff, internal and external consultants, and parents to gather their perspectives and suggestions for accomplishing the goals.

- Honor the dates you established to review progress on the goals and the overall plan. Being fully accountable to the plan will keep everyone on track.

- Add a sense of fun, joy, and happiness to the process. Applaud small accomplishments and plan larger celebrations for substantial achievements.

As described in chapter 3, a thoughtfully crafted IPDP helps teachers articulate their goals and then take the appropriate steps to achieve them. Leaders can use this same system to create a program improvement plan. The following case study shows how one program overcame the obstacles to its success by creating processes that involved full staff participation.

Reflective Practice Exercises

CASE STUDY: GREAT KIDS EARLY CHILDHOOD PROGRAM

Great Kids Center was facing a myriad of challenges: high staff turnover, communication issues between staff and administration, a lack of focus on curriculum, and low staff morale. In order to effect lasting change it was essential that the staff be involved in each step of the creation of the program improvement plan.

Creating a vision statement that was inclusive of and meaningful to the large staff required a multi-step process. Two all-staff meetings were held. At each meeting, the teachers and administrators participated in reflective activities that provided the foundation of the vision statement. The first meeting included a brief overview of vision statements, and staff watched the powerful movie *Celebrate What Is Right with the World* by Dewitt Jones (www.celebratewhatsright.com/film). A series of reflective activities followed.

Reflective Activities

Gathering in small groups, staff members considered the film's ideas and the following reflection questions to spark discussion.

> *If I really wanted to soar, that was the edge I had to push—that edge in each of our lives between success and significance . . . Could I do that? Could I trust myself, my values, and my vision enough to step out beyond my own edge?*

> —Dewitt Jones

- In what ways are you now ready to push forward beyond your own edge to soar?
- If you were granted three wishes to bring your professional vision for your work at Great Kids to life, what would they be?
- What resources and support will you need as you step out beyond your own edge?
- How can you start to put into practice "I won't see it 'til I believe it"? How would this approach help to strengthen the learning community here at Great Kids?

Each group used chart paper and markers to record the key points of their discussion. After forty minutes of vibrant discussions, the groups presented their key ideas to the large group.

After these short presentations, the groups got back together to complete a focused appreciative inquiry exercise involving the following scenario, questions, and challenge.

You fall into a deep sleep and wake up refreshed. It is one year later and you are an active, engaged staff member at Great Kids, and the program is operating at its best:

- What is going on that engages you fully?
- What is contributing to its success?
- How are you incorporating your creativity, strengths, and your three wishes?

As creatively as possible, describe, draw, or perform a skit, a rap, or a song that captures the essence of your engaging program. Each group will share their collective dream.

These skits were the highlight of this all-staff meeting. Humor was combined with rich descriptions of each group's vision for creating a vibrant, engaged program.

The meeting wrapped up with a focused discussion of this question: What are the key areas of growth for Great Kids based on what was shared tonight?

After the meeting, the leadership team gathered to review the large amounts of information that staff members had shared through the reflective activities.

Creating a Vision Statement and Goals

A second professional day was planned with the key goal of creating a shared vision statement and drafting goals for a programwide professional development plan.

The second all-staff meeting started off with discussions of a word cloud and vision boards.

To build a connection between the work done at the first session, facilitators created a word cloud from all the words the group used to describe their three wishes for the program. We used the online tool Wordle (www.wordle.net) to create the visual, and everyone received a color copy. I facilitated a discussion around the key words and themes that appeared in the word cloud.

Organizers asked each participant to bring a vision board that reflected their hopes and dreams for the program when it was operating at its highest level of quality. (See the overview of vision boards in chapter 2.)

The teachers and administrators shared their vision boards in small groups. Then each group shared the key words that emerged from their discussion, and they created a master list of key words and common themes as shown in the table that follows.

Key Words	Common Themes
Creative	Culturally sensitive
Collective	Healthy and safe
Nurturing excitement	Fun—joyful—happy
Supportive	Community
Flexible	Culture
Diversity	Holistic
Compassionate	Developmentally appropriate
Innovative	Fully staffed—knowledgeable, competent
Respectful	Teacher time—planning, collaborating, problem solving
	Opportunities for growth—children's enrichment, professional development, visiting other schools
	Communication
	Money for raises and resources
	Respectful treatment—staff to staff, staff to admin, admin to staff, empathy, open mindedness
	Clear, consistent expectations and accountability

These key words were used to draft and redraft a vision statement that reflected the hopes and dreams of teachers and administrators. By the end of the second staff meeting, the team had created a rough draft of the key points to include in the vision statement. The administrative team used these key points to draft three vision statements and asked staff to comment via email and at team meetings. Using the staff comments, the team finalized the vision statement, deciding on the following:

> Our vision is to create a thriving learning environment that deeply respects and nurtures the potential that exists in each child, teacher, and family. Through ongoing collaboration and open communication we will establish a vibrant community where joy, learning, creativity, and meaningful relationships flourish.

Engaging teachers in the powerful process of creating a programwide vision statement builds momentum for all that is possible. Participants in this process have shared some of the following comments:

- "We got to talk about the real stuff of wanting to collaborate and be more connected."

- "I enjoyed hearing everyone's ideas. We shared so many wonderful ideas about children and families."

- "We have touched on creating more community building between classrooms in the past. This is the first time I feel it will happen!"

Part two of the second all-staff meeting was an interactive activity designed to produce a first draft of the specific goals needed for bringing the vision to life. In the hallway, we posted large pieces of chart paper with an area from the eight Massachusetts Core Competencies listed on the top of each sheet:

1. Understanding the growth and development of children and youth

2. Guiding and interacting with children and youth

3. Partnering with families and communities

4. Health, safety, and nutrition

5. Learning environments and curriculum

6. Observation, assessment, and documentation

7. Program planning and development

8. Professionalism and leadership

Using the core competencies as a framework helped to guide the groups in creating goals that would focus on quality in all aspects of the program. Working in small groups that mixed teachers with administrators, the groups brainstormed goals and specific improvement activities that they felt would help the Great Kids program achieve its newly drafted vision. After the small groups were finished, a large group discussion allowed participants to review and condense the goals and action steps.

The leadership team used all the information from this activity to shape the following goals and action steps for the program development plan:

- Provide a rich, meaningful, developmentally appropriate curriculum that meets the individual needs of the children, and have the resources to implement the curriculum.

- Create a staff supervision model that includes an administrator who supports curriculum development in the classrooms.

- Strengthen the curriculum component of the program in all classrooms.

- Support a teaching staff that feels empowered and has a larger voice in the program.

- Create new ways to share the skills and expertise of each staff member to strengthen the organization.

- Develop a new staff meeting protocol that is inclusive of teachers sharing their expertise and areas of interests.

- Build respect for diversity of teaching styles.

- Develop clear organized goals for the program and all individuals working in the program that will guide the continued growth of the program.

- Establish a code of ethics and hold all individuals in the organization accountable to it.

- Utilize the IPDPs for the program and the staff to create a system of clear expectations and accountability throughout the program.

- Develop a clear organizational chart that is understood by all stakeholders in the organization.

- Utilize data from assessment tools (Teaching Strategies Gold, CLASS, Arnett, Strengthening Families, PAS) and yearly evaluations from parents and teachers to continually assess the program's strengths and areas of growth.

- Have a renewed, positive, optimistic energy that is evident in all aspects of the program.

- Have a leadership team that is fully engaged with promoting and modeling collegiality in meaningful ways across the organization.

- Staff are fully invested in their own learning and professional growth.

- Improve and utilize existing space and materials to create a fresh, clean, clutter-free, and inviting environment.

- Support a vibrant parent community that is based on mutual respect and inclusive of all families.

These goals and action steps formed the foundation of a detailed action plan that refocused and reenergized the program to enhance all aspects of quality. The program leaders felt strongly that they now had a road map that would help them align with the new quality initiatives (QRIS, NAEYC, and state licensing). Through their active participation, teachers felt valued, respected, and engaged. The administrators and teachers at the Great Kids program then began actively working through one goal at a time. The program has been making consistent progress, and that in turn has had a positive effect on the work environment for teachers and the education of the children in the program.

 *Align!*

Including Required Components in Your Program Improvement Plan

Program improvement plans can follow a variety of formats depending on the requirements of the quality initiatives they are associated with. The categories for the plans generally include:

- Goals that are clearly stated and measurable

- Detailed action steps that support improvement in program quality

- Individuals responsible for each action step

- A specific time frame for completing each action step

- Resources needed (such as money, time, materials, or people)

- Benchmarks for success, with links to specific data as relevant

- Dates for review of the plan

The format for developing program improvement plans can vary according to each state's requirements. Check with the agency that supports your QRIS to see if you need to use a specific format.

Observations and Feedback

The program development plan led to considerable shifts in how the leadership team supervised teachers. The team realized that their old ways of working with teachers were no longer effective. In order to totally rethink how they were supporting teachers, the leadership team worked together to re-create their supervision model. They reviewed their current model to see what was working and what was not, and researched other early childhood leadership models. After an intensive process, they created a unified system that aligned their supervisory responsibilities and leadership tasks. A major shift involved changing their leadership model so every administrator had a specific group of teachers to supervise. They then defined the supervisory responsibilities of each member of the leadership team.

This process helped the team realize they were missing a critical element—support for Great Kids' educational and curriculum component. With some budget adjustments they were able to develop a plan to hire a skilled educational leader to support the teachers and the leadership team in this key area. Under the curriculum coordinator's guidance, they were able to develop protocols for observing teachers and giving them consistent feedback.

Incorporating Data

This program had many sources of data available, much of which had been gathered specifically for the requirements of quality initiatives such as NAEYC accreditation or QRIS. However, putting all the program data on the table and incorporating it into their program development plan was a new process for the leadership team. As they carefully reviewed and analyzed the data from the PAS, NAEYC Family Survey and Teacher Survey forms, Teaching Strategies Gold, Infant/Toddler Environment Rating Scale, ECERS, and CLASS, the team gained a whole new perspective on the strengths and challenges of each area of their program. This process provided insights into the areas they needed to address and prioritize in their program improvement plan. The team became fully committed to reviewing data from the same tools to assess their growth.

As the data review continued, the leadership team realized that they were missing a key piece of information. They had no clarity on the specific goals of the teaching staff. Knowing that this information would guide them forward, they set a tight time frame for each supervisor to meet with their assigned teachers to compile a current IPDP. Once the IPDPs were completed, they created a master list of goals that they needed to support. This one-page summary was an important reference point for their ongoing work with teachers. (See Appendix C: Vision and Goals Summary.)

Strategic Professional Development

The program improvement plan was instrumental in designing a yearlong professional development calendar. This was the first year that the program had taken an intentional approach to organizing relevant and meaningful professional development. The leadership team reviewed the vision, program goals, data, and each teacher's IPDP goals to create a master list of areas to weave into their professional development work. The comprehensive calendar included specific needs-based training sessions for four full professional days, plus monthly staff training sessions aligned with specific recommendations to address the unique needs of individual teachers. Being intentional, focused, and strategic about the use of professional development time and budgeted funds helped to support lasting growth in the areas of identified needs.

Focused Check-In Meetings

To keep the leadership team energized and focused, administrators scheduled two leadership retreats during the school year. These retreats included time to assess where progress was being made and identify new strategies for supporting other areas. They were essential in keeping the program on track.

The program leaders reassessed their progress at the end of the first year and moved forward to create a revised plan to guide them through year two.

Embracing Quality Changes in Early Childhood Programs

Once the program improvement plan is created, it will guide leaders in how they prioritize their time, allocate funding, enhance curriculum, strengthen instructional practices, and select meaningful professional development experiences that are directly linked to improvement goals. These plans represent a major shift in how leaders lead. Instead of waiting for something to go wrong and then trying to fix it, leaders can become proactive and find ways to improve outcomes for all children in their program. Stepping forward to educate young children in ways that honor and respect their full potential requires educators who are passionately committed to continuous quality improvement.

CHAPTER 5

Igniting Passion through Engaged Leadership

Energy is one word that I have seen that differentiates great leaders from average leaders. Great leaders not only have positive energy, they contagiously spread this positive energy to others.

—Bruce Schneider, *Energy Leadership*

The ever-increasing focus on consistently improving the quality of early childhood programs creates the need for passionate leaders who bring positive energy into all facets of their work. The skills needed to lead early childhood programs in this era of standards and accountability are vastly different from the skill sets required of leaders in the past. It is time for leaders to become active protagonists who guide and inspire their teachers to embrace the changes necessary to support the holistic growth and development of the children in their care.

Many directors have spent years developing the skills needed to successfully manage and oversee their programs—budgets, enrollment, facilities, teachers, parents, and curriculum. For some administrators, moving from a managerial approach of leadership to a more pedagogical approach can seem daunting. This shift can occur gradually by embracing one new idea or leadership strategy to begin the process of creating the ongoing changes needed for lasting programmatic transformation.

In all aspects of leadership, unwavering positive energy is required to facilitate long-term changes. As directors have begun navigating their way through the new quality initiatives, I have seen two patterns of behavior emerge. The first is to face new requirements and expectations with negativity and grim determination. These directors manage the paperwork process efficiently, but engagement with the teachers is often low. Nancy, a longtime director of a large child care program, shared with me the difficulties she was having getting her teachers to embrace the programmatic changes required of them. She sent out endless emails, posted lists of required staff changes in the staff room and gave directives during staff meetings about the changes she wanted to happen. When speaking with Nancy, she freely shared a steady stream of complaints about her staff: "What's wrong with them? Don't they understand we will lose our funding if they don't do what I tell them? Can't they see the mess we are in?" Her negative perspective permeated all aspects of the program.

Nancy was aware that she focused little time or energy on directly engaging with the teachers. When I asked her about the time she spent in directly interacting with teachers for classroom observations and feedback sessions, she told me that the teachers did not even know when she was doing the required observations. This seemed improbable to me until she explained that she used the video camera monitors on her desk to do the observations. She then filled out the required form and placed it in the teacher's file without ever discussing the observations with or providing feedback to the teacher.

Nancy's story is a stark example of how some directors are attempting to meet new expectations without building positive relationships with their teachers, thereby limiting the likelihood of staff investment or commitment. Although this director's system for observations was not benefiting her teachers or meeting the intent of any standard, she felt she was keeping up with the requirements. Nancy's low level of engagement with the teachers around the new expectations and standards was an unintentional catalyst for the negative reactions of the teachers and their unwillingness to change.

The second pattern has been an upsurge in energy and a commitment to become a stronger program that is aligned with quality. Stephanie, an executive director of a multisite program, is an excellent example of bringing positive energy into the large and often overwhelming task of aligning with a new quality initiative. Stephanie had shared with me that she had some philosophical difference with the new quality initiatives in her state. She struggled with how she could fully embrace the initiative when she felt conflicted by some of the requirements. Although Stephanie could see many of the benefits of the initiatives, she was delaying participating due to her strong belief that a couple of standards needed to be modified. After a period of uncertainty, Stephanie found the energy to use her experience and expertise to advocate for change in her role as an experienced early childhood administrator. She got involved with the process by finding constructive ways to advocate for changes: she joined a statewide advocacy organization, testified at a public hearing, and wrote letters to state officials. These actions were empowering and actually built the positive momentum Stephanie needed to bring the new initiative into her program. When Stephanie decided to fully participate in the initiative she took a positive approach in communicating her commitment to the process. She knew she did not want her specific concerns to create a negative cloud over this process and she wanted to honor the strong, trusting relationships she had with her staff. She sent out the following inspirational letter to the leadership team of her programs.

> *Hi Everyone,*
>
> *You will be receiving a packet of documents that will help us expedite our application to the QRIS. There is a time line with it—I am working on my accountability skills.*
>
> *Imagine this: A family walks into your center and says "I have heard so much about the Children's Garden. You have a reputation throughout the town for offering children and families the best in child care and early learning. I loved your website. It was so informative and the children and teachers look so happy. I also know that the state has implemented a new Quality Rating Improvement System. I was thrilled to learn that the state also recognizes the Children's Garden as offering exemplary education to children."*
>
> *Our rating in the QRIS system will soon be public. We deserve to be rated highly by the state. We know we are great, and now it is time to put some muscle behind it and prove it!*
>
> *Join me in presenting the best of the Children's Garden—you and your teachers—to the public!*
>
> *Be the center of your dreams!*
>
> *Stephanie*

It is often easy to find fault with an aspect of the many standards, initiatives, and regulations that are part of the early childhood world at this time. This fault finding can lead you down a path of disengagement and negativity that can hinder your ability to inspire staff to embrace the necessary changes. Stephanie's story shows us that it is possible to move past our own conflicting thoughts and create a positive alignment with the quality initiatives as a way to highlight your program's vision and spark the energy needed to get the wheels of change in motion.

Leaders who are passionate, intentional, and fully engaged will be able to facilitate the continuous quality improvements necessary to keep pace with the new standards and initiatives designed to improve child outcomes. The following strategies provide new perspectives and resources for shifting to a more positive and inspirational leadership style.

Multiplying Individual Strengths

The style and methodologies leaders use can have a profound impact on everyone who works with them. To support programs on the journey to higher levels of quality, successful leaders find a variety of new ways to tap into the unique strengths and talents of every individual working with them. In this way, leaders can multiply the intelligence of colleagues in powerful ways that bring renewed energy and full engagement to the entire program.

Stephanie and Nancy represent profoundly different leadership styles. Stephanie is able to demonstrate inspirational leadership, embrace change, visualize success, and impart a can-do attitude. Stephanie's leadership style reflects Liz Wiseman's description of a *multiplier* in her book *The Multiplier Effect*: "A leader who uses their intelligence to amplify the smarts and capabilities of the people around them. People get smarter in their presence because they're given permission to think. These are the leaders who inspire employees to stretch themselves to deliver results that surpass expectations. These leaders seem to make everyone around them better and more capable."

Nancy, on the other hand, has a leadership style that shuts down positive energy, and individual and organizational growth. Her negative outlook and lack of engagement with staff contribute to a high-stress environment. It is apparent that Nancy fits Wiseman's description of *diminisher*: "They are smart leaders, but they shut down the smarts of others. They are idea killers and energy zappers. They create pressure and stress that can shut down ideas for good."

The affect that these two different leadership styles can have on performance is illustrated in the Align! box on page 78. Multipliers, described as "genius makers," are so successful at bringing out the best in each employee that they tend to be able to coax 2.3 times the capacity from an individual that a diminisher can. How does this relate to early childhood programs? When you are able to shift your leadership style to being a multiplier, you can amplify the strengths and passions of each teacher so they become more fully engaged with teaching and being active members of the school community. Making this shift will help you move out of the negative spiral of complacency, where low energy and low levels of engagement quickly become the norm.

Becoming a multiplier requires you to reflect on your own practices and make changes that will support others in being their very best. Consider some of the tips that follow as you strive to reach this goal.

Discover the very best in each of your staff. What are their innate talents and skills? What brings them joy and happiness? How do they shine? Why were they hired? What do parents value most about them? What do their coworkers value most? Even if the staff member has a challenge or growth area that needs to be addressed, it is crucial to see the person's strengths. This Jon Gordon quote captures the essence of this important process: "Dust on gold doesn't change the nature of the gold. It's still gold . . . the key is to realize that inside everyone is gold that wants to shine. The value is on the inside. Help them find their gold." When you acknowledge the treasures each person brings, you will find your staff more willing to brush off the dust and bring the very best of who they are into the program.

Create opportunities for all colleagues to use their talents, passions and strengths to benefit the program. Allowing every staff member to share her unique areas of expertise will reinvigorate the program and enable the whole community to recognize and value their colleagues in a new light.

Be inclusive. The early childhood workforce is made up of individuals of diverse race, gender, ethnicity, age, and educational backgrounds. Take the lead on embracing diversity. Spend time getting to know each person. Learn about their interests, skills, and dreams to better support their professional growth in meaningful ways. Raise your own consciousness and find new ways to respect the values and beliefs of the individuals you work with.

Step aside and make room for others to lead. Be willing to let others shine and allow them to be seen for their strengths. Who could share their expertise by presenting at a staff meeting? Who could become a mentor for other teachers in their area of strength? Who could provide a new perspective on an administration challenge you are facing? People love to contribute their talents and expertise. By allowing them to do so, you'll acknowledge and validate that they are respected for all that they bring to the program.

Share leadership. Being seen as the only decision maker contributes to a negatively viewed top-down culture. Find opportunities for the teachers to have a voice in the decision-making process to build trust, respect, and a strong sense of community. Some ideas to start this process:

- Pose questions at staff meetings in ways that give colleagues a chance to authentically contribute ideas. A way to quickly brainstorm is to give small groups a question modeled after the top ten lists on the *Late Show with David Letterman*: Top ten ways we could improve the quality of our program? Top ten ways we could enhance our literacy work with children? Top ten ways we can get parents more actively involved? Have the groups share their answers with the large group and then facilitate a discussion around all that is possible.

- Invite staff to be active on committees and provide multiple opportunities for them to be involved. Be willing to support them as they stretch into this role. Encourage their participation, ask them to prepare something to share with the committee, and provide them with strengths-based feedback on their contributions.

- Encourage expertise sharing. Support staff members in sharing their ideas, talents and resources with each other. Create forums for this to happen formally and informally. Stretch staff to develop a workshop or training for educators outside the program. Local NAEYC chapters and other early childhood organizations host local conferences that are an ideal forum for teachers to share their expertise with others.

- Stop fixing everything! Leaders often feel they are being helpful by swooping in to fix the problems that occur throughout their programs. Fixing actually diminishes other people's confidence in their own competence. Give your staff the mentoring and resources they need to solve their own problems in ways that increase their self-efficacy.

As you continue to work to be a multiplier, periodically reflect on the ways you might be shutting down the expertise of others. Many leaders don't realize that some of the actions that they believe are supportive actually hinder the growth of others. If you would like to discover more about your leadership tendencies, you can take the accidental-diminisher quiz on the Multipliers Books website (http://multipliersbooks.com/multipliers/take-the-quiz/).

Practicing Mindful Leadership

In the midst of the swirling activity that is ever present in early childhood programs, leaders must develop strategies to keep themselves grounded and focused. Janice Marturano, author of *Finding the Space to Lead*, captures the importance of bringing mindfulness into our lives: "We can no longer afford to be on autopilot in our lives, with our families, or in our organizations. We can no longer afford to miss the connections with those we work with, those we love, and those we serve. We can no longer make decisions with distracted minds, reacting instead of responding or initiating. We need mindful leadership to lead with excellence."

Mindful practices are essential for guiding leaders out of a state of disequilibrium to a place of calmness. Jon Kabat-Zinn, the founding executive director of the Center for Mindfulness in Medicine, Health Care, and Society at the University of Massachusetts Medical School, defines mindfulness in this way: "Mindfulness means paying attention in a particular way: on purpose, in the present moment, and nonjudgmentally." Like so many professionals in our fast-paced world, early childhood leaders are often so caught up in worrying about what hasn't been and what needs to be done that they are missing out on the only moment we can truly shape—the present.

In a 2010 article in *Harvard Magazine* written by Cara Feinberg, Harvard University psychology professor Ellen Langer describes mindfulness as "the process of actively noticing new things, relinquishing preconceived mindsets, and then acting on the new observations." However, Langer notes

 Align!

Understanding the Differences between Diminishers and Multipliers

	Diminishers	
	These leaders are absorbed in their own intelligence, stifle others, and deplete the organization of crucial intelligence and capability.	
SEE	**The Assumption** "People won't figure it out without me."	
DO	**The Five Disciplines of the Diminisher**	
	The Gate Keeper	Hoards resources and underutilizes talent
	The Tyrant	Creates a tense environment that suppresses people's thinking and capability
	The Know-It-All	Gives directives that showcase how much they know
	The Decision Maker	Makes centralized, abrupt decisions that confuse the organization
	The Micromanager	Drives results through their personal involvement
GET	**The Result** **40%**	

	Multipliers	
	These leaders are genius makers and bring out the intelligence in others. They build collective, viral intelligence in organizations.	
	The Assumption "People are smart and will figure it out."	SEE
	The Five Disciplines of the Multiplier	DO
	The Talent Finder	Attracts talented people and uses them at their highest point of contribution
	The Liberator	Creates an intense environment that requires people's best thinking and work
	The Challenger	Defines an opportunity that causes people to stretch
	The Community Builder	Drives sound decisions by constructing decision-making forums
	The Investor	Gives other people ownership for results and invests in their success
	The Result **2.3X**	GET

Source: Wiseman, Liz, Lois Allen, and Elise Foster. 2013. *The Multiplier Effect: Tapping the Genius inside Our Schools.* Thousand Oaks, CA: Corwin. Reprinted with permission.

The results noted in this figure refer to the capacity that leaders can draw out of colleagues. According to research by Wiseman, Allen, and Foster, diminishers tend to get only about 40 percent and multipliers tend to get about 88 percent of employees' capabilities. The detailed figures translate to multipliers drawing about 2.3 times more intelligence from those they lead. The different leadership styles are marked by the assumptions and disciplines the leaders employ in working with others.

that most of the time our behavior is mindless. When leaders move from mindless behavior to be being fully present in their work, they create more meaningful connections, increase their creativity, and are able to focus on all that is possible. Mindfulness promotes the overall health and wellness that leaders need to inspire and guide others.

Small changes can result in major shifts in approach. The following chart will provide some starting points for you to begin to incorporate mindfulness into your day.

Simple Mindfulness Tips	Practices That Cultivate Mindfulness
Breathe! Take three deep breaths	Meditation
Start each day with a quiet moment	Yoga
Focus on what is going right—create a win list	Some martial arts
Reduce noise and clutter	Spending time in nature
Play	Spending time away from technology
Speak kindly	Self-observation to increase awareness

Recharging Your Energy by Reclaiming Time

Without effective time-management skills, early childhood leaders can find themselves exhausted, stressed, and overwhelmed by the demands of their work life. The added pressures of implementing new quality initiatives have increased stress and left leaders struggling to get it all done. Become more mindful of how you use your time throughout the day to gain insight into how you can reclaim time for what is truly important.

Responding to immediate needs, large and small crises, and constant interruptions has become part of the everyday life of school leaders. When these day-to-day issues are escalated to an urgent level, it is often the result of poor planning or procrastination. Consequently, everyone involved feels an energy shortage. Stephen Covey aptly describes this situation as "urgency addiction." He describes what happens when you constantly work in crisis mode: "Some of us get so used to the adrenaline rush of handling crises that we become dependent on it for a sense of excitement and energy. How does urgency feel? Stressful? Pressured? Tense? Exhausting? Sure. But let's be honest. It's also sometimes exhilarating. We feel useful. We feel successful. We feel validated. And we get good at it . . . It brings instant results and instant gratification."

Living in a constant cycle of responding to crisis after crisis wears leaders down. The symptoms of burnout, including exhaustion, frequent illnesses, self-doubt, and feelings of ineffectiveness, begin to settle in. School leaders need to empower teachers to manage confidently the day-to-day issues that will inevitably arise. To help teachers become more self-reliant, and to better support their program, leaders need to spend less time in crisis mode and more time on the crucially important tasks of relationship building and thoughtful planning.

It's an ongoing challenge for leaders to become more focused and intentional about how they spend their time. Because planning tasks are perceived as not urgent, they often become overlooked. The reality is that when leaders plan their time, they can create space in their days to achieve the fundamental tasks that help teachers to feel fully supported to develop the skills, competence, and independence they need to be successful. As teachers' needs are met through positive interactions that acknowledge and validate their strengths, they are less likely to escalate small issues into crises as a means of getting attention and support. When leaders succeed at meeting the needs of the teachers in their program, they can dramatically reduce the crisis-driven behaviors that drain leaders.

Like the proverbial sand in the hourglass, the minutes and hours of our professional days can slip away, and we find that we have not accomplished what we set out to do.

To create more time for what matters most, leaders must look carefully at how they are spending their time. A leader who gets caught up in dealing with constant interruptions often finds it impossible to achieve her goals and support the professional development needs of her teachers. For early childhood leaders, these activities alone could fill their daily schedules. Parents dropping in, teachers with questions, deliveries, phone calls, and the constant ding of new email all create a sense of urgency for things that are not necessarily urgent. Strategic leaders find ways to create peaceful, focused times in their days to concentrate on the work that supports ongoing growth and strong relationships. Closing the office door at scheduled times each day, shutting off email notifications, and limiting unnecessary meetings will help to reclaim time that can be better spent elsewhere.

A time log is an important reflection tool for leaders to begin thinking about how they spend their time and what changes they can make to better support their vision and the professional growth of teachers. Leaders who take one week to diligently complete the time log at the end of this chapter will gain a better understanding of where their time goes. Once the log is completed, leaders can move on to the important part—analysis.

Carefully review your logs and use the data to find answers to these questions:

- What percentage of your time is directly linked to your vision and goals? To supporting the goals of teachers?

- How much time is lost to interruptions?

- What people did you spend your time with? What does your time spent with these individuals represent?

- How are urgent situations affecting your time?

Then reflect on strategies for making intentional changes:

- How can you make changes that will increase your ability to use your time so that you are working to bring your vision to life and achieve your goals?

- What ideas do you have for minimizing interruptions?

- How could the time and energy being spent on urgent situations be reduced?

- How could you find new ways to spend time with the people who need your presence the most?

- What new systems could be put in place to maximize your efficient use of time?

- What could you delegate?

When leaders become fully aware of how they are using every precious minute of their workdays, they can make the shifts needed to better align their use of time with their vision and goals.

Practicing Self-Care

Leaders are notorious for spending every ounce of energy they have taking care of the needs of others. As selfless as this may seem to you as a leader, it is actually a disservice to everyone that you work with. Running around in a frazzled state will prevent you from being the calm, reflective, and empowering role model that teachers, children, and families need. One of the most relevant metaphors for self-care is said daily on airlines: "Put your own oxygen mask on first!" If you allow yourself to become depleted, then you will not have what you need to help others. Take time each day to be sure that you get enough rest, nutritious meals, moments of peace and relaxation, exercise, and social and intellectual stimulation. It is not selfish; it is essential. When leaders bring the best of who they are to their leadership roles, they have the focus and clarity to embrace all aspects of their work.

Leaders who push themselves to deal with too many demands on their time and energy can end up with minor issues becoming large-scale problems, as the following scenario illustrates. Greg, a director of a preschool, was having an unusually stressful start to the school year. He was dealing with training new teachers, a complicated board issue, and a medical situation in his own family. Greg knew one of the teams was not settling in to a healthy work relationship. When Greg shared the degree of discomfort he was feeling regarding this team with me, I asked how he planned to rectify the situation. His response reflected his lack of energy: "I just want them to make it through the school year. I don't have the energy to deal with this."

Greg's lack of engagement with this issue allowed the situation to escalate to the point that a family filed a complaint with the state licensing agency, laying out the details of the high-stress environment in which their child was being cared for. This complaint and the subsequent investigation proved to be a wake-up call for Greg. He was fully aware that his lack of engagement and hands-off approach to dealing with this classroom team issue allowed it to escalate.

To his credit, Greg blamed no one but himself. Once the complaint investigation was over, Greg knew that taking care of himself was the first step in finding the energy to get his program back on track. He realized that working long hours, not taking his vacation time, and trying hard to take on all the extra projects that the parent advisory board members felt were necessary had reduced his ability to focus on the crucial aspects of his job. This honest self-reflection helped Greg to develop a work schedule focused on his key priorities and create a work-life balance that allowed him to come to work each day refreshed and ready to fully engage in his work.

Practicing self-care does not have to be a daunting task. A first step is to be fully aware of what is draining you. The Clean Sweep diagnostic assessment is a good place to start. It guides you through personal questions that will give you clarity on key areas that you would like to strengthen to feel less stress. You can access the Clean Sweep assessment on the CoachVille website (http://www.coachville.com/tl/thomasleonard/cleansweeppdf.pdf).

Reflective Practice Exercises

Take some time to reflect on ways that you might improve your energy for leadership; the strategies that follow provide some options for insight and planning.

CREATING A WIN LIST

Directions: Think about all the amazing moments that happen daily in your work life. Create a list of ten wonderful experiences that have brought you joy, happiness, and professional satisfaction. Complete the win list as often as necessary to refocus your thoughts. Some people do this daily; others find once a week is most helpful.

This strategy will help you develop the habit of focusing on what is going well and what you truly value in your daily work. As you shift your focus from what is wrong to what is right, you should find that your level of positive energy increases.

CLUSTER WRITING

Directions: Gather three blank sheets of paper, and write the words *engaged leadership* in the center of the first page and then draw a circle around the words. Take two minutes and create a word map (one option is a web graphic organizer) of everything that comes to mind when you think of engaged leadership. After two minutes take the last word or phrase you wrote and place that in center of page two. Create a word map based on that new starting point. Repeat these steps for your third piece of paper. Without fail, this process helps release new thoughts and ideas. You might also try repeating the process with the words *mindful leader*, *multiplier*, *energy leadership*, and *appreciative leadership* as your starting point to gain insights into your own thoughts for enhancing your leadership.

TIME LOG

Directions: Accurately record all aspects of your day, even the time-wasting activities that may seem insignificant but can add up to a large amount of time. Make a new entry whenever you switch activities. Pay careful attention to whom you are spending time with, urgent situations that drag you away from your scheduled activities, and interruptions that occur. A detailed time log will give you data you can reflect on to decide what changes you would like to make in how you are using your time.

Sample Time Log

Time	Activity	Scheduled	Interrupted	Urgent	People Involved	Comments

CHAPTER 6

Facilitating Effective Professional Development

Generations of teachers have continued to undergo their initial preparation and in-service professional development without ever having reflected on the range of things we know about learning and on the relationship of learning with the context. And especially, forgoing any research for new ways, new languages, that could enable teachers to live, share, narrate and perform learning events.

—Carlina Rinaldi, *In Dialogue with Reggio Emilia*

Reflective practice and continual professional development are vital to transforming the quality of early childhood programs. Amid external pressures for quality improvement, effective leaders can use the internal strengths of their programs to promote positive changes. As a school leader, think about how you can gain a new perspective to facilitate the professional growth of your staff.

The first shift in approach is to move beyond simply completing a set number of hours to satisfy a local or national standard. For many teachers and leaders, completing professional development has been focused on finding courses and workshops that help them meet the required hours or courses, without considering how to link the training to their professional goals. To have the greatest impact on growth in professional practice, you can guide each teacher to find the most relevant learning opportunities that address their individual professional needs and specific goals.

The second shift requires school leaders to be intentional in the planning and delivery of professional development experiences that will improve the educational practices of their staff. Michael

Fullan, in his article titled "Why Teachers Must Become Change Agents," states, "It has long been known that expertise is central to successful change, so it is surprising how little attention we pay to it beyond one-shot workshops and disconnected training." The following steps will lead to professional development that is directly linked to the goals of the program and of the specific teachers and administrators working in the program:

1. Carefully review the vision and the goals outlined in the program's continuous quality improvement plan and the individual professional development plans for all teachers and administrators. This will help you determine the key areas of growth for the program and provide a framework for cohesive professional development planning for your leadership team and teachers.

2. Create and complete a template that concisely lists the goals for the program, administrators, and teachers so you can stay focused on those goals as you plan each professional development experience. (See Appendix C: Vision and Goals Summary.)

3. Be sure that program goals and teacher goals align with state standards and competencies so that professional development offerings address the full range of skill needs in your program. (See Appendix D: Sample IPDP Summary Sheet.)

4. Once the goals for professional development are clear, leaders can move forward and schedule meaningful learning opportunities that will lead to professional growth in the areas of most relevance. (See Appendix E: Sample Professional Development Planning Sheet.)

A third shift is establishing a common language for the terminology of professional development. In response to the need for consistent definitions, NAEYC and the National Association of Child Care Resource and Referral Agencies jointly developed a glossary of terms, which is summarized in the Align! box that follows.

Align!

Professional Development Terms

- *Early childhood education professional development* is a continuum of learning and support activities designed to prepare and enhance educators' work with and on behalf of young children and their families. The goal is to improve the knowledge, skills, practices, and dispositions of early education professionals.

- *Professional development* encompasses education, training, and technical assistance.

- *Individual professional development plans* (IPDPs) are documents that connect various professional development experiences to each other and to the common core of knowledge and professional standards for early education professionals.

- *Training* is a learning experience, or series of experiences, specific to an area of inquiry and related skills or dispositions, delivered by professionals who have expertise in the subject matter and adult learning.

- *Technical assistance* is targeted and customized support provided by professionals who have expertise in the subject matter and in adult learning. This support is intended to develop or strengthen processes, knowledge application, or implementation of services by recipients.

- *Mentoring* is a relationship-based process between colleagues in similar professional roles, with a more-experienced individual with adult learning knowledge and skills, the mentor, providing guidance and example to a less-experienced colleague, the protégé or mentee.

- *Coaching* is a relationship-based process led by an expert with specialized and adult learning knowledge and skills, who often serves in a different professional role from the recipient. Coaching is designed to build capacity for specific professional dispositions, skills, and behaviors, and is focused on goal setting and achievement for an individual or group.

- *Consultation* is a collaborative, problem-solving process between an external consultant with specific expertise and adult learning knowledge and skills and an individual or group from one program or organization.

Source: National Association for the Education of Young Children, and National Association of Child Care Resource and Referral Agencies. 2011. *Early Childhood Education Professional Development: Training and Technical Assistance Glossary.* Washington, DC: NAEYC.

As you look for ways to foster growth among your program's staff and achieve lofty goals, find ways to incorporate learner-centered approaches to professional development that will increase engagement.

Engaging in Reflective Practice

Reflection provides avenues for educators to continually refresh their perspectives, but the idea is not new. John Dewey captured the essence of reflective practice back in 1910 in his book *How We Think*: "Reflection is turning a topic over in various aspects and in various lights so that nothing significant about it shall be overlooked—almost as one might turn a stone over to see what its hidden side is like or what is covered by it." Developmental insights surface when leaders allow time and space to engage in reflective practice with teachers. Often, what teachers need most from leaders is someone to guide them in discovering, or in some cases rediscovering, their strengths and connecting with the areas that they want to fully develop.

Hearing first-hand from workshop participants the insights they have gained through the reflective practices that I weave into every presentation is inspirational. One of the most profound experiences I witnessed was with Laura, a college course participant who appeared disengaged through the first few sessions of the course. To encourage course participants to create a meaningful vision for their career path, I pose a provocation for them to craft a visual representation of their vision, as I did with Laura's group. A *provocation* is simply an item or items designed to provoke interest, invite creative thinking, and encourage the formulation of ideas. I brought in stones, dried flowers, sea glass, ribbons, symbolic items, and a placemat for each participant. With soft music playing, each participant created her own vision and then shared it with the group. I was deeply struck by the beautifully articulated vision statement that Laura shared. She spoke with a strong sense of conviction about her desire to finish her bachelor's degree and then her master's degree, so that she could lead the program she was currently working in. When I spoke with her at the break, I asked her what would have happened if I had assigned her to write a vision statement as a homework assignment. Would she have written the same thing she shared in class? She responded that she would not have had clarity about her future if she had not had time to think and create her vision with the materials. Providing rich provocations and time in quiet reflection can help teachers improve self-awareness, tap into new thoughts, and communicate ideas in new ways.

The reflective process allows for individuals and groups to take different vantage points to get a new perspective and broader understanding. It is an ongoing process that adds depth and meaning to professional development opportunities by increasing dialogue and engagement around issues of growth and change.

The following model illustrates the process of looking strategically, thinking deeply, and responding with a fresh perspective.

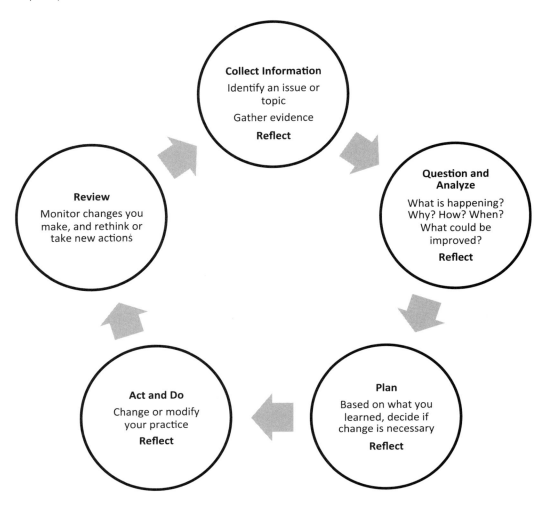

The Reflective Process Graphic

Source: Adapted from: Kennedy, Anne, and Anne Stonehouse. 2012. *Victorian Early Years Learning and Development Framework: Practice Principle Guide 8 Reflective Practice.* Melbourne, Australia: State of Victoria Department of Early Childhood Education. http://www.education.vic.gov.au/Documents/childhood/providers/edcare/practiceguide8.pdf

Leaders can support reflective practice by using a variety of supervisory and training techniques, including case studies, journals, portfolios, analysis of video or audio clips, and small learning groups focused on action research or book studies. Giving individuals the rich opportunity to become protagonists in their own learning will create powerful shifts in their professional practice.

Incorporating Multiple Intelligences

In early childhood classrooms, educators often use Howard Gardner's theory of multiple intelligences to create engaging learning experiences. Somehow, this practice is much less commonplace—although just as relevant—in the creation of adult learning experiences. Gardner has identified eight distinct intelligences:

- **Verbal-linguistic:** Sensitivity to the meaning and order of words

- **Logical-mathematical:** The ability to handle chains of reasoning and to recognize patterns and order

- **Musical:** Sensitivity to pitch, melody, rhythm, and tone

- **Bodily-kinesthetic:** The ability to use the body skillfully and handle objects adroitly

- **Visual-spatial:** The ability to perceive the world accurately and to re-create or transform aspects of that world

- **Interpersonal:** The ability to understand people and relationships

- **Intrapersonal:** Access to one's emotional life as a means to understand oneself and others

- **Naturalist:** The one who is able to recognize flora and fauna, to make other consequential distinctions in the natural world

The multiple intelligences also provide a framework for tapping into the unique skills and abilities of teachers. When you recognize that adults learn in different ways, you can tailor professional development to educators' diverse strengths instead of presenting traditional lecture-style workshops. The table that follows shows examples of training activities that relate to each of the eight intelligences.

Professional Development Attuned to Multiple Intelligences

Professional Development Activity	Multiple Intelligence Type
Role playing and skits	Verbal-linguistic, interpersonal, visual-spatial, musical
Group discussions	Verbal-linguistic, interpersonal
Hands-on experimentation	Kinesthetic, logical-mathematical
Journal writing	Intrapersonal, verbal-linguistic
Constructing timelines	Logical-mathematical, visual-spatial
Building a model or 3–D display	Kinesthetic, logical-mathematical
Ropes courses, outdoor team-building exercises	Naturalist, kinesthetic, logical-mathematical
Create documentation panels	Visual-spatial, verbal-linguistic
Write and perform a song, rap, poem, or nursery rhyme	Musical-rhythmic, verbal-linguistic
Brainstorm responses in groups	Linguistic, interpersonal
Watch video clips in small groups and respond using reflective protocols	Visual-spatial, linguistic, interpersonal

Understanding and Supporting Adult Development

Early childhood teachers enter the profession with diverse education and work experiences. To best support each teacher, reflect on their stage of development before determining the most appropriate methodologies.

Lillian Katz identified four stages of development for early childhood educators in her article "Developmental Stages of Preschool Teachers"—survival, consolidation, renewal, and maturity.

Teachers in the survival stage are trying hard to develop the skills to get through their day. They are figuring out the routines of their classroom and of the school, learning to interact with colleagues and parents, and trying to meet the needs of each child. This is a period of time where heightened feelings of anxiety and inadequacy can surface. Supporting teachers at this stage requires a balance of empathy and specific skill development. On-site guidance and direction from a supervisor, curriculum specialist, or behavior specialist can best support the professional development needs of these teachers.

In the consolidation stage, educators have built up some confidence and know that they are competent enough to survive. Katz characterizes these teachers as "ready to consolidate the overall gains made during the first stage and to differentiate specific tasks and skills to be mastered next." Educators tend to reach the consolidation stage after their first year of teaching, and they still greatly benefit from ongoing supervision. Peer collaboration and the ability to interact with internal and external specialists are other ways these educators can develop and deepen their knowledge.

Educators tend to enter the renewal stage during their third or fourth year as educators. They now have confidence in their pedagogical practices and begin to look outside the classroom and program for new ideas and inspiration. Teachers at this stage often show boredom at doing the same things over and over. They are looking to bring new energy and passion into their work. You can support teachers in the renewal stage by getting them out to see other programs; connecting them with new research, videos, and books related to their interests; having them attend conferences; and encouraging them to join professional associations.

Some teachers take three years to reach the maturity stage, and others take five or more years. Teachers at this stage begin asking deeper, more philosophical questions. Katz provides examples: "What are my philosophical roots? What is the nature of growth and learning? How are educational decisions made? Can schools change societies? Is teaching a profession?" Educators in the maturity stage benefit greatly from participation in college courses, regional, and national conferences, study groups, and book groups, and they respond well when given opportunities to interact with other teachers.

Understanding these stages will help you to best meet the needs of individual educators and align resources that can help them continually grow and develop.

Establishing Strong Pillar Practices

Through her extensive research with school leaders, Ellie Drago-Severson, a professor of education leadership and adult learning and leadership at Teachers College, Columbia University, has identified pillar practices that support transformational learning and growth: teaming, providing opportunities for leadership roles, conducting collegial inquiry, and mentoring. These practices can build collaboration, provide opportunities for reflection, and deeply engage teachers in their own professional growth.

TEAMING

Leaders can find meaningful opportunities for educators to work in teams to support the program. Teamwork can help adults feel safe to share their views and challenge one another's thinking. That provides fertile ground for growth. Working in teams can build educators' confidence, reduce isolation, improve interpersonal skills, and allow educators to feel they are contributing to the school community in significant ways.

It's crucial that leaders get to know each teacher's strengths, passions, interests, and skills. When educators are invited to join teams that interest them and allow them to stretch their skills, professional growth will follow. Opportunities for teaming include participating in committees (for example, curriculum or technology), having a small group of teachers collaborate to create presentations for staff meetings and parent events, and organizing groups of teachers to work with parents on school improvement and beautification projects. The key is to build collaboration and provide authentic experiences to support professional growth.

PROVIDING OPPORTUNITIES FOR LEADERSHIP ROLES

Wise leaders share leadership. Encourage teachers to share their strengths, talents, and skills outside of their classrooms. This is an often-overlooked way to increase their self-efficacy and spark intrinsic motivation for ongoing professional growth. When teachers are invited to take on a leadership role, no matter how small, it sends them the clear message that their individual strengths are recognized and valued by their school leader. As teachers take on leadership roles, their ability to see themselves as professionals is strengthened. I experienced a surge in professional confidence in a young teacher in my program when she began helping me edit the school newsletter. She had excellent writing skills, and I wanted to find a way to strengthen our relationship. Working with her in the office just an hour a week helped her to feel valued as a professional and gave me time to connect with her in a collegial way. School communities benefit from the collaboration, respect, and trust that are developed when leadership is shared. No matter how big or small, every school has a multitude of opportunities for teachers to use their unique areas of expertise to step into leadership roles: board liaison, parent tour coordinator, photographer, videographer, curriculum specialist (in their area of strength), librarian, interior designer, gardener, blog or newsletter editor, marketing specialist, and supply coordinator. The more you know about teachers' strengths, the easier it will be to create an opportunity for them to feel confident and capable in leadership roles.

Conducting Collegial Inquiry

Collegial inquiry engages educators in thoughtful dialogue that can help them share their own perspectives and broaden their own views by listening to and learning from the assumptions, beliefs, and perspectives of their colleagues. You might engage educators in the inquiry process by asking them to reflect on a provocative question, write an individual response, and discuss those thoughts in small groups. Another example would be to hold a conflict-resolution meeting in which participants are asked to reflect on a problem, suggest solutions, and discuss possible options for moving forward. Thinking about varied approaches, analyzing and discussing differences, and formulating shared solutions can foster active engagement that leads to growth and change.

Mentoring

When an educator can use her expertise to support the development of another teacher, both the mentor and mentee can gain a renewed sense of dedication, professional pride, and energy for growth. Mentoring can take many forms; most commonly, an experienced teacher mentors a new teacher. But every teacher and every school is different. Your staff might get more out of mentoring if you match teachers based on strengths, not just seniority. A new teacher who has strong technology skills can support a colleague in developing new ways to bring technology into the classroom. Partnering her with a long-term teacher who can mentor her in the operational policies and procedures of the program creates an opportunity for them both to grow and learn from each other. Consistently providing opportunities for all teachers to share their knowledge and skills will benefit everyone.

These practices encourage collaboration, build a vibrant, supportive school culture, and create meaningful ways for participants to think deeply about their experiences to improve their own competence and professional growth. These practices can be seamlessly integrated into early childhood programs without the added costs of hiring external consultants, trainers, or mentor coaches.

Leading Engaging Meetings

Leaders have the ability to influence the professional growth of their educators at every staff meeting. In many programs, however, staff meetings are focused on the mundane operational issues involved in managing a school. The meetings are often dominated by the director with minimal staff participation and engagement. If you choose to put transformational change at the top of your agenda, you can make time for that by communicating about day-to-day updates and announcements in weekly emails or memos distributed to all staff. If programmatic issues needs to be discussed with the group, reserve the last ten or fifteen minutes of the staff meeting for that business, after you have given full attention to the higher-level focus of the meeting.

To increase engagement and build collaboration, leaders can promote the establishment of group norms. For educators to want to participate in meetings, they need to feel that they can safely express their views. Parker Palmer has worked with his team of facilitators at the Center for Courage and Renewal to develop touchstones for creating safe spaces. Consider using these touchstones, outlined in the Align! box, as a resource for supportive group discussions..

Intentional Plans for Staff Meetings

Staff meetings that support professional growth need to be intentionally planned around a clear goal. Review your list of program goals and individual teacher goals to help you determine the key topics you want to address at your staff meetings. Use a planning sheet to lay out the focus of each meeting and how it will meet the needs of your staff. (See Appendix E: Sample Professional Development Planning Sheet.) Encourage teachers and assistants to suggest topics for staff meetings, too. Send out a survey with questions related to staff members' professional development needs, interests, and ideas to help them feel integrated into the planning process. Online survey tools such as Survey Monkey (https://www.surveymonkey.com/) and Zoomerang (http://www.zoomerang.com/) make creating, distributing, and tabulating surveys a quick-and-easy process.

Plan your agenda to incorporate reflective practices and provide opportunities for exploration and active participation. The following agenda items make a good starting point.

WELCOME AND OVERVIEW

Begin by providing a warm welcome to staff members. They are often coming to these meetings after a long workday. Beautify the meeting space with tablecloths, flowers or plants, displays of books, or photos of materials relevant to the meetings. Have water and small snacks available.

# Align!

Setting Meaningful Guidelines for Safe Group Interactions

Although you can use these guidelines as standard operating procedure, they do not follow conventional meeting protocols but rather take a more sensitive approach. Parker Palmer calls these key points *touchstones* because you should return to them over and over during group discussions to the keep interactions grounded in a safe space that promotes trust.

- Extend and receive a welcome.

- Be fully present.

- Participants offer contributions by invitation, not demand.

- Speak your truth in ways that respect your colleagues' truths.

- Don't try to fix, save, advise, or set each other straight.

- Respond to colleagues with honest, open questions.

- When discussions get sticky, turn to wonder.

- Listen to your inner teacher.

- Preserve deep confidentiality.

- Know that you can get your needs met.

Let people know the structure and focus of the meeting. Honor their time by keeping on track. Jot reminders on sticky notes about items that need to be discussed later, and attach them to your planner or to a whiteboard. Talk about them at the end of the meeting, if there is time, or commit to following up at a later date.

REFLECTIVE OR CENTERING ACTIVITY

A short reflective activity allows teachers to shift their focus to the main topic of the meeting. Share relevant poems, quotes, images, or a children's book, and then ask the teachers to respond. Depending on the size of the group, participants can share in pairs, in small groups, or with the whole group. Sample reflective activities are listed at the end of this chapter.

PRESENTATION AND DISCUSSION OF KEY ISSUES

Keep presentations short, engaging, and interactive. Encourage teachers to prepare and present topics at the staff meeting. They might present on educational practices, classroom management techniques, or technology; share new and interesting resources; present a challenging situation as a case study; share a tool for documentation; or discuss any area of interest that they feel confident sharing. Keep slides and other presentation aids simple and visually appealing. Limit the amount of text, and use relevant photos and images to relay your points.

Be sure to incorporate reflective questions throughout the presentation. If you ask probing questions—such as "How does this relate to your work in the classroom?" or "What do you find interesting or challenging about this?" —you are more likely to keep teachers focused and reduce boredom.

OPPORTUNITY TO PRACTICE APPLYING IDEAS

The real learning in any staff meeting happens when teachers fully engage with the topic. Teachers need time to interact with each other and—when possible—with a variety of materials to deeply integrate the new knowledge into practice. Case studies, provocations, role plays, and group work all provide rich learning experiences. No matter how fabulous the presentation is, participants will have most of their aha moments when they are actively engaged in their own learning.

CLOSING AFFIRMATIONS

Take a few minutes at the end of every meeting to have teachers identify an action item. This supports educators in taking the relevant information from the meeting and bringing it into practice. Affirmations are stated in the positive and are written in the present tense—as if the goal is currently happening. Have index cards available for teachers to write their affirmation statements on and encourage them to place their cards somewhere that they can look at the affirmations daily. A reflection sheet for writing affirmations is provided in Appendix B.

EVALUATIONS AND FEEDBACK

Give teachers the opportunity to share feedback after each meeting. Use the feedback to continually enhance the meetings and let teachers know how much you value their thoughts and input.

A powerful example of the impact that feedback can have on teachers' growth happened after a parents' night event where the teachers presented stories of the work happening in their classrooms. This was the first time that teachers were taking on the role of presenters, and the teachers were feeling stressed and insecure going into the meeting. They did a remarkable job sharing their work, and parent engagement was high. When I reviewed the evaluation forms, I knew this was important information to share with the teachers. At our next staff meeting we reviewed the feedback and had a rich discussion about how much the parent community values their commitment and passion as educators. Here are some examples of the parents' comments:

- "I thought the teachers put together and made a great presentation. Their passion for the process, and more importantly, for children and childhood was wonderful to see."

- "I learned a great deal, but more importantly for me: I felt warmth and genuine commitment to the welfare of each child."

- "It was eminently clear that each of the teachers not only loves what she does, but really believes she is living her 'dream job.'"

- "The integrity and generosity of spirit that I witness daily as a parent were present. It was thoughtful, welcoming, and engaging. I felt part of the community too, in the same way I know my own daughter feels."

Reflective Practice Exercises

To keep your professional development sessions interesting, interactive, and engaging, you need to use a wide range of training techniques and activities. The following list of some of my favorite training activities will get you started in developing a tool box full of new ideas.

CREATING EMPOWERING VISION SCULPTURES

Ask participants to create sculptures of rocks, glass beads, ribbons, dried flowers, and symbolic items to capture the essence of their own vision. This can be used to help participants share their thoughts about their own professional growth or to capture their vision for the program's growth. Provide a brief description of the focus:

- Create a vision sculpture that reflects your professional aspirations. Pick a time frame—one, two, or three years—and then use words and images that reflect what your ideal professional life will be at that point in time.

- Create a vision sculpture that reflects our program operating at its highest level of quality. (Can be done individually or in small groups.)

- Create a vision sculpture that reflects what will be happening in our program when we achieve accreditation or the highest level of quality awarded by our state's QRIS. (Can be done individually or in small groups.)

Have participants share their vision sculptures and discuss common themes as a group. (An additional vision exercise is located at the end of chapter 2.)

Your Image of the Child

Ask participants to read the article "Your Image of the Child: Where Teaching Begins," by Loris Malaguzzi and to bring a photo or picture that captures each person's image of the child to the workshop or meeting. Start the meeting by having each participant share his picture and discuss why it reflects his image of the child. This article is available for download at: https://reggioalliance.org/downloads/malaguzzi:ccie:1994.pdf

Hopes and Dreams

This simple activity (described in detail in chapter 1) has a profound impact on building community and allows everyone to hear their colleagues' diverse views. Give participants index cards, and ask them to write their hopes and dreams for the coming year. Collect the cards, and then randomly pass them back to the participants and ask them to read the cards out loud. Discuss common themes.

This activity works for both teacher groups and parent groups. These cards provide invaluable quotes that can be used in newsletters or blogs and to spark reflective conversations at meetings. The words and sentiments from these cards can also be woven into an end-of-the-year photo montage as a way to reinforce how the stated hopes and dreams came to life in the program.

Brainstorming and Letterman's Top Ten

Brainstorming is a powerful activity that helps to get many voices heard on a particular issue or topic. I find participants get very engaged when the brainstorming is framed like the top ten lists on the *Late Show with David Letterman*: Divide participants into small groups. Provide each group with a large blank sheet of paper, some markers, and a prompt that starts with Letterman's Top Ten [fill in the blank]. The opportunities are endless, but a few ideas include: Letterman's Top Ten Ways . . . to Improve the Quality of Our School, to Engage Children in Project Work, or to Create More Collaboration Between Teachers and Classrooms. Have each small group share their top-ten list with the entire group. Then debrief by discussing common themes that came up. Use a timer and play some game-show music to add a sense of playfulness to this activity.

Quotes and Poems

As an opening reflection, select a poem or quote that has meaning and relevance to the topic of the meeting. Carefully select poems and quotes that represent a variety of points of view and diverse cultures. I often offer a selection of quotes on a particular topic and then ask the participants to select one quote that resonates with them and have them share it with the group. There are many Internet sites that can help you compile lists of quotes and poems that are meaningful and relevant.

Children's Books

Linking children's literature into professional development provides rich opportunity for discussions and reinforces the importance of reading books. The book should be relevant to the focus of the training. If it is a long book, select a section to read that is most meaningful. One book that provides participants the opportunity to deeply reflect on their own childhood and the importance of creating lasting memories for children is *The Big, Big Sea* by Martin Waddel. Comb your book shelves or stop by the local library to gather books that will be useful for supporting professional growth.

Provocations

When teachers can explore with materials, they increase their engagement and tap into many of their multiple intelligences. Natural items, such as rocks, moss, shells, flowers, and sticks, add beauty and a sense of calmness to activities. Set up a visually appealing display of natural items, and then ask teachers to use the materials to create a visual depiction of their vision for their work in the next two years, or the story of their career path in the early childhood field. Allowing teachers to use materials to tell the story creates a richer, deeper, more meaningful experience.

The power of provocations is that they help individuals to tap into their own creativity to express their thoughts, ideas, and feelings. The possibilities for provocations are endless, and many fabulous materials are readily available in early childhood programs. Using art materials, clay, wire, blocks, sand, collage materials, and collections of found items will create rich hands-on learning experiences for teachers.

Music

Using music during workshops helps to set the tone of each activity. Each session is unique, so try to build a playlist of music that you can draw on depending on the activity and the makeup of the group. To set a welcoming tone, play calm, peaceful music as the group gathers. Playing energy-boosting music helps people refocus after a break. It's fun to add game-show music and sound effects to the group activities. A few high-energy songs that encourage dancing are great for short energy breaks. Play music during reflective activities to help keep participants focused and engaged with their writing. I often observe that participants seem to be writing to the tempo of the music. To add music into your workshops, simply try out one or two songs and see how they affect the group. Thousands of songs are available, so start with a few of your favorites and build up your playlist gradually.

Photos and Video Clips

Just as you teach to different learning styles in your classrooms, remember to do the same in your workshops. Using photos and video clips varies instructional delivery and can help attendees to retain even more of what they've learned. Incorporating reflective activities, individual questions, and group discussions after viewing photos or videos is a powerful way to facilitate rich dialogues and the exchange of ideas between participants. Visual images of other programs, a teaching methodology, behavior management strategies, and learning environments can allow teachers to see beyond their everyday life in their classroom and develop a broader perspective on the early childhood field. A wide range of free video clips is available on YouTube (https://www.youtube.com/) and TED talks (https://www.ted.com/talks). Videatives (https://videatives.com) offers a variety of short video clips with descriptive texts, specifically designed for use in training early childhood educators. School leaders and teachers can create in-house video clips and use them to gain insights into their own practices. Align the video clips with the key goals for the workshop so they will strongly influence the professional growth of the teachers.

Supporting and developing staff members are top priorities for program leaders. The ongoing development of teachers is a continual process. Having a tool box full of effective professional development ideas and resources will prove to be invaluable as you work toward that goal. The creativity and passion that leaders model in the design of their professional development opportunities will provide sparks of energy and increase momentum for teachers to unleash creativity and passion in their classrooms.

CHAPTER 7

Using Strengths-Based Coaching Techniques to Increase Engagement

Too often we underestimate the power of a touch, a smile,
a kind word, a listening ear, an honest compliment, or the
smallest act of caring, all of which have the potential to turn
a life around.

–Leo Buscaglia, *Love*

Strengths-based coaching represents a new approach to solving the energy-draining problems of low staff engagement and a lack of motivation for incorporating high-quality educational standards into daily practice. Gallup Poll data released in January 2016 reveals that only 32 percent of U.S. employees were engaged at work in 2015, 50.8 percent were not engaged, and 17.2 percent were actively disengaged. Lack of full engagement by teachers and administrators in early childhood programs has a negative impact on all facets of program quality, including outcomes for children, staff turnover, the culture and climate of the program, and commitment to professional growth. Factors that contribute to engagement include having a leader who encourages an employee's development and recognizes his strengths.

Educational leaders have struggled with the effectiveness of their supervisory roles for decades. Earle Connette, in his 1937 article "A Questionnaire for Supervisors" states: "No longer we can bide our time doing the many things we have done in the past and feel assured that we are really supervising. Indeed, on the whole, we have erred!" His statement, made over 75 years ago, is as true today as it was then! The following questions, adapted from his article, provide powerful reflection points for early childhood leaders:

- Is my supervision cooperative and democratic or do I act in ways that signal domination and dictatorship?

- Do I systematically check in with each teacher, or do I trust to past experience that what I have shared will be beneficial?

- Do I suspend judgment about a teacher's issue until I have completely assessed and analyzed the situation, or do I base the need for improvement on casual observations?

- Do I supervise the teaching, or do I leave that responsibility up to teachers who may not be following what I view as best practices?

- Do I hold a meeting with collegial input, or do I dominate the meeting?

- Do I encourage competent teachers to carry on research individually or in groups, or do I think I am the only one with that capability?

These questions follow a specific pattern that is representative of an ongoing leadership challenge—the first part is strength based and the second part is deficit based. In the book *Evocative Coaching*, authors Bob Tschannen-Moran and Megan Tschannen-Moran note that inspiring leaders recognize that "it is easier to outgrow problems when teachers focus on their strengths, vitalities, and aspirations. Both adult learning theories and growth-fostering psychologies support this approach. Research indicates that appreciative, strength-based inquiries are more effective and empowering than analytic, deficit-based inquiries." In other words, when teachers feel that their strengths are recognized, they become inspired to take action for further improvement. As a leader, you can promote that kind of positive atmosphere.

The Focus of the Coaching Process

Coaching is a profession that has many definitions, often depending on who is being coached (athlete, corporate executive, or educator). The following thoughts on coaching highlight the powerful impact it can have.

- Sally Zepeda in her annotated bibliography on performance coaching: "Coaching is concerned with empowerment and the development of potential. Effective coaches know when and how to stretch, when and how to challenge, and when and how to guide those whom they are coaching. The prerequisites of coaching are collaboration and trust in order to develop and to achieve goals and objectives. Coaching for results takes into account the needs of the organization as well as the experience, maturity, knowledge, and career path of the individual. To this end, coaching is developmental and differentiated, relying on adult learning and career stage theories."

- Dathan Rush and M'Lisa Shelden in *The Early Childhood Coaching Handbook*: "An adult learning strategy in which the coach promotes the learner's ability to reflect on his or her actions as a means to determine the effectiveness of action or practice and develop a plan for refinement and use of the action in immediate and future situations."

- Bob Tschannen-Moran and Megan Tschannen-Moran in their book *Evocative Coaching*: "Coaching is a conversational process that brings out the greatness in people. It raises the bar of the possible, so that people reinvent themselves and their organizations in the service of transformational learning."

Note the common thread in these definitions—they use words such as *trust, reflect, conversational, transformational*, which are hallmarks of positive relationships. Strengths-based coaching is thus a relationship-based professional development activity that can produce some of the following benefits:

- Higher levels of well-being and confidence

- Energy, effectiveness, productivity, and a sense of meaning

- Conscious awareness that promotes growth

- Appropriate developmental growth in children

- A broader perspective

- Enhanced confidence and a stronger sense of identity

- Use of best practices in the classroom

- Improved staff supervision skills

- Lower levels of staff turnover

- Higher levels of program quality

- Improved administrative skills, including fiscal management, building partnerships with families, and board relationships

- Greater career satisfaction and fulfillment

With the opportunity for such strong gains in program quality, it is crucial for you to develop coaching skills. These skills help you build trusting relationships that ultimately will engage teachers in their own professional growth.

Characteristics of Effective Coaching

To effectively coach the educators in their programs, directors need to understand adult learning theory, reflective practices, and the fundamental principles of coaching. In *The Early Childhood Coaching Handbook*, Rush and Shelden identify five practices that will help the coach and protégé achieved intended outcomes:

- **Joint planning**—Engage teachers in planning a focus for their coaching.
- **Observation**—Observe the teacher during activities directly related to the area of focus.
- **Action and practice**—Support the teacher in carving out opportunities to practice and refine skills.
- **Reflection**—Use reflective questions to analyze the current situation and identify possibilities for continued growth.
- **Feedback**—Provide comments and dialogue that affirm and validate the teacher's knowledge and skills.

Although most directors are using some of these practices—observation, for example—it is important to use all five practices to fully support and develop teachers' skills. The International Coach Federation has established a set of eleven core competencies that coaches generally need. The Align! box that follows highlights nine of the competencies that can benefit school leaders specifically as they coach teachers.

Each competency has the potential to enhance the coaching relationship between the director and teacher. Together they can infuse the coaching efforts with energy that can drive quality improvements.

Transforming the relationship between directors and teachers from boss and employee to inspirational leader and engaged teacher is at the core of creating quality improvements in the early childhood field. Your coaching challenge is to create a relationship built on shared goals, trust, open conversations, and a focus on strengths. With a professional yet comfortable atmosphere, you can encourage your teachers to see possibilities that can breathe new life into their efforts for self-growth and result in improved teaching and learning.

Strengths-Based Coaching Strategies

It takes courage to leap into a new approach when working with teachers. The transition to a more strengths-based approach can be a gradual process of trying out new techniques. The positive results will build the momentum you need to embrace this new way of leading and supporting teachers.

Developing Skills for Successfully Coaching Teachers

- Establishing respect and trust through a supportive environment

- Projecting a coaching presence that is confident and a style that is open and flexible

- Engaging in active listening by focusing on the teacher's words, underlying meaning, and the context of the discussion related to the teacher's goals

- Using powerful questions that promote clarity, discovery, and insight

- Engaging in direct communication that clarifies and reframes the teacher's points in respectful ways

- Creating awareness by promoting inquiry and discussion, sharing other perspectives, examining interpretations, and encouraging analysis

- Collaboratively designing actions that promote exploration of new ideas, deeper learning, self-discovery, and successful experimentation

- Developing a coaching plan with the teacher, including setting goals, making adjustments, and finding early success targets

- Managing progress by making clear requests, checking in on actions, providing feedback, and holding the teacher accountable for following through

Source: International Coach Federation. 2016. "Core Competencies," accessed May 13, 2016. http://www .coachfederation.org/icfcredentials/core-competencies

LISTENING

The power of listening cannot be understated, yet it is often a huge challenge for leaders to shut out the constant humming and swirling of thoughts that inhabit their offices and their minds, in order to practice effective listening skills. In the book *Strength to Your Sword Arm*, Brenda Ueland captures the deep impact that listening can have: "Listening is a magnetic and strange thing, a creative force . . . When we are listened to, it creates us, makes us unfold and expand. Ideas actually begin to grow within us and come to life . . . When we listen to people there is an alternating current, and this recharges us so that we never get tired of each other . . . This little creative fountain inside us begins to spring and cast up new thoughts, and unexpected laughter and wisdom . . . It is when people really listen to us, with quiet, fascinated attention, that the little fountain begins to work again, to accelerate in the most surprising way."

Creating time and space to listen with fascinated attention is the key to establishing respectful relationships. When leaders do this they can build, or in some cases rebuild, the sense of trust that is necessary for strengths-based relationships to be established and for the process of transformation to begin. Through listening we can move beyond our own judgments and limiting perceptions. Carlina Rinaldi in her chapter in *The Hundred Languages of Children*, provides a unique perspective on the impact that listening has in school communities: "Peace is a way of thinking, learning, and listening to others, a way of looking at differences as an element of connection, not separation. Peace is a way of remembering that my point of view is not the best, and I need to hear and understand others' points of view. Here is where we find the roots of participation in the school as a place to encounter differences. We must have the courage to share and to disagree. Listening provides the opportunity for professional and human development."

Developing listening skills may appear to be a simple task, but it takes practice to move away from the established norm of multitasking. Teachers and leaders are caught up in the mentality that tells us we have to keep going full speed ahead, while dealing with the distractions of constantly flowing information and demands for continuous communication, so that we do not fall behind. The reality is that our inability to succeed is linked to not being present and attentive in the moment. Being present to fully hear what someone is saying requires us to raise our consciousness beyond all that distracts us. Multitasking sends the clear message that we are not listening and that the individual is not important enough to warrant our full attention. Taking a moment to pause, clear our minds, put down our electronic devices, and give our attention to another person is one of the most important gifts we can give. The mnemonic *WAIT and SEE*, which Nicola Stevens suggests in her book, *Learning to Coach*, can be a helpful tool. Reminding yourself what WAIT and SEE stands for can help you refocus on listening.

> WAIT: Why am I talking?
>
> and
>
> SEE: Stop explaining everything!

Another helpful reminder is a word play on *SILENT*—when you switch the letters around you can spell *LISTEN* and *ENLIST*. It is important to remember to silence our internal voice as well as all external distractions and enlist our ears and minds if we want to truly be present, deeply listen, and connect with each other.

Psychoanalyst Ralph Roughton, M.D., captures the essence of the importance of listening in a nonjudgmental way. All too often leaders rush in to fix others' problems, when in reality all that is needed is to be a good listener.

"Listen"

When I ask you to listen to me, and you start giving advice,

you have not done what I asked.

When I ask you to listen to me and you begin to tell me

why I shouldn't feel that way, you are trampling on my feelings.

When I ask you to listen to me and you feel you have to do something to solve

my problems, you have failed me, strange as that may seem.

Listen! All I asked was that you listen—Not talk or do . . . just hear me.

When you do something for me that I can and need to do for myself,

you contribute to my fear and inadequacy.

And I can do for myself! I'm not helpless;

maybe discouraged and faltering, but not helpless.

But when you accept as a simple fact that I do feel what I feel, no matter how

irrational, then I can quit trying to convince you and can get about the business

of understanding what's behind this irrational feeling.

And when that's clear, the answers are obvious and I don't need advice.

Irrational feelings make sense, when we understand what's behind them.

Perhaps that's why prayer works, sometimes, for some people . . . because God is

mute and He or She doesn't give advice or try to fix things.

God just listens and lets you work it out yourself.

So, please listen and just hear me. And if you want to talk,

wait a minute for your turn, and I'll listen to you.

Source: Reprinted by permission of Ralph Roughton, M.D.

ENGAGE IN APPRECIATIVE INQUIRY

In order to engage in strengths-based coaching, leaders need to shift their focus away from the negative and onto the positive. This shift takes a conscious effort for many leaders who have spent years leading from a deficit-based perspective. When leaders focus on what's wrong they unintentionally create a school culture focused on what's wrong. A tremendous amount of time and energy is spent working with individuals, teams, and the entire staff to discuss what is wrong. This deficit-based approach drains energy, promotes a negative identity and culture, and shuts down creativity.

To promote lasting improvements, leaders need to focus on the strengths of the program. The appreciative inquiry approach is built on the *heliotropic principle*, which is that what we shine the light on grows. Leaders who continually shine the light on what is wrong create a more negative environment and increase resistance to positive change. It is up to you to stay out of the negative spiral that can envelop your program and look for the positives in all situations to nurture growth.

Diana Whitney, Amanda Trosten-Bloom, and Kae Rader, in their inspirational book, *Appreciative Leadership*, describe five core strategies for unleashing positive potential. These strategies, outlined in the Align! box that follows, provide a solid framework for early childhood leaders to bring strengths-based coaching techniques into their daily work.

Their book describes the compelling impact of appreciative leadership as "the relational capacity to mobilize creative potential and turn it into positive power—to set in motion positive ripples of confidence, energy, enthusiasm, and performance to make a positive difference in the world." This description captures the true benefits of fully aligning with a strengths-based approach to leadership—an increase in passion, engagement, and motivation.

A vivid example of the power of illuminating strengths is my coaching relationship with Dolly, a family child care provider, whom I was assigned to coach as part of a QRIS grant that she received. When I first visited Dolly, she seemed totally confused by my role and was resistant to coaching. She was so resistant that she would not allow me into her family child care home. For the first two sessions, I sat in her backyard on a folding chair and she spoke to me through an open bulkhead door while the children slept. After the second session, I offered to bring my camera with me so I could take before and after photos of her space. Dolly was receiving a large equipment grant, and from our conversations I knew she was excited about the changes to the space. When I arrived at her home for the third session, she did let me in to take the photos. As I entered, I immediately understood her resistance to letting me in. The space was poorly lit and cluttered with an old fish tank and a big broken television. The linoleum was peeling off the floor in spots.

As a coach who is deeply committed to having a strengths-based approach, I knew I was facing a major challenge. I took a few deep breaths to focus myself and settled myself into the task of taking photos. Watching Dolly through the camera lens helped me to see her true strengths. The way she looked at the children and spoke to them was truly magical. Her love for the children was evident

Align!

Embracing the Core Strategies of Appreciative Leadership

Strategy	Actions	Impact
Inquiry	Ask positively powerful questions	Lets people know you value them and their contributions
Illuminate	Bring out the best in people and situations	Helps people understand how they can best contribute
Inclusion	Engage with people to coauthor the future	Gives people a sense of belonging
Inspiration	Awaken the creative spirit	Provides people with a sense of direction
Integrity	Make choices for the good of the whole	Lets people know that they are expected to give their best for the greater good and that they can trust others to do the same

Source: Reprinted with permission from: Whitney, Diana Kaplin, Amanda Trosten-Bloom, and Kae Rader. 2010. *Appreciative Leadership: Focus on What Works to Drive Winning Performance and Build a Thriving Organization.* New York: McGraw-Hill.

through her kind words, the gentle way she touched them, the games she played, and the sweet songs she sang. Taking the time to truly see Dolly and appreciate all that she brought to the lives of the children in her care proved to be the pivotal turning point in our relationship. When I was getting ready to leave, I told Dolly, "These children are so lucky to have you to love them."

By illuminating Dolly's strengths I was able to connect with her in a profound way. In an instant, she became more relaxed and comfortable with me. She asked me to sit with her at the kitchen table and she shared her dreams of creating a beautiful environment for the children to play in. She truly wanted the best for these children, all of whom were in care through state-funded protective care slots. Our coaching relationship blossomed as soon as trust was established, and we were able to work together to transform her child care environment.

The most significant change was Dolly's confidence in herself. At our last session, she shared how she had taken her old equipment and helped another provider, who had not received a grant, redesign her space. Dolly's pride at how she was able to help the children in her care, as well as their parents and other providers, was a remarkable transformation from the frightened, shy woman who spoke to me through her bulkhead door.

THE FOUR-QUESTION PROTOCOL

The appreciative inquiry four-question protocol provides a simple and inspirational framework for school leaders to use when building strengths-based conversations with teachers.

- **Best experiences**—Formulate questions to tap into each individual's story of their unique best experiences: "What was your best experience as a teacher in the four-year-old classroom? What was your best experience dealing with a child with challenging behaviors? Or a challenging parent? Why do you consider this example your best experience?" Urge teachers to describe their experiences in detail.

- **Core values**—Engage in conversation about what the individual deeply values. "What do you value most about your role as an educator? What led you to choose early childhood education as your career? What brings you the greatest source of pride in your work?"

- **Supporting conditions**—Focus on what helps educators be at their very best. "When you think about the best year you had as an educator, what helped you to be at your best? What were the internal and external factors that contributed to your success? What supports, resources, or guidance would you need to have your best year of teaching in your current position?"

- **Three wishes**—This playful question helps educators think about all that is possible. "If you could make three wishes come true that would transform your teaching practice, what would they be? If your three wishes for your teaching magically came true overnight, what would be different in your classroom the next day? What would you be doing? What would the children be doing? How would the environment of the classroom be different?"

This is a generic protocol, meaning that it can be adapted to fit the individual and the situation that is the focus of coaching. By taking the time to customize the questions to align with the specific professional goals and needs, you can unleash positive energy that is often dormant. When leaders are successful in helping teachers reconnect with their strengths, they will see an increase in their self-efficacy and motivation for growth and positive change.

ASK EMPOWERING QUESTIONS

When leaders ask empowering, strengths-based questions, they set the tone for positive engagement. This simple, yet powerful, technique is a perfect place for leaders to begin creating the small changes that will lead to lasting results. One place to start is to replace the standard "How's it going?" or "How are you doing?" with the energizing question "What's the best thing that has happened to you today?" Questions like this take conversations away from the stagnant greetings and dialogues and add new energy and focus to our ongoing dialogues. Remember that empowering questions are questions that we can't possibly know the answers to. Adding one or two new questions into your repertoire each week will help you gradually incorporate the questions into your daily conversations. Here is list of twenty empowering questions to get you started:

- What would you like to learn to do really well?

- What brings you joy?

- What gets you truly excited about your professional work?

- What motivates you to do your very best?

- What do you want to spend more of your time doing each day?

- How can you make the best of this situation?

- What is the most effective thing for you to focus on?

- What do you need to be successful in this program or classroom?

- Why do you get up in the morning and come to work?

- Who is a role model for your work as an educator?

- How has this role model influenced your teaching?

- What would you do differently next time?

- What would make your professional life more wonderful for you?

- How would you describe your future in three words?

- How can you share your gifts and talents?

- What is your intuition telling you about this situation?

- How can you make your work more fun?

- What do you need more of?

- How will you celebrate your success?

- What are you seeing that I am not?

TRANSFORM NEGATIVE CONVERSATIONS INTO AFFIRMATIVE TOPICS

Early childhood leaders are faced with a multitude of negative issues each day. Teachers often stop by the office to share a tale of woe involving their personal life, a challenge with a staff member, or a situation with a child. Parents also frequently drop in with concerns and complaints. The way a leader responds to these resoundingly negative conversations can shape the outcome. By using positive questions, leaders can become successful at transforming negative discussions into positive ones. The authors of *Appreciative Leadership* describe this powerful process as "the flip" and lay out three steps for moving from negative conversations to affirmative questions:

1. Listen to the complaint carefully. Restate your understanding of what you heard.

2. Ask the other person what outcome they would like. What resolution are they seeking?

3. Reflect the desired outcome you heard in a brief, affirmative way. This is the point that turns the conversation around, or flips it.

Leaders are often faced with habitual complainers, who challenge the leader by bringing up the same or similar negative issues again and again. By flipping the conversation toward a positive orientation, leaders can get beyond the complaint and find out what the individual truly wants. Practicing this process will help leaders transform conversations away from the draining energy of negativity and support positive outcomes.

Build Confidence in Teachers' Competence

Teachers need to know that you see their strengths even during challenging times. As a leader, your challenge is to look past the negativity expressed in the moment and connect with the unique passions and skills the teacher is capable of bringing to the program.

To best support professional growth, identify the areas that the teacher is succeeding in. By identifying the areas of best practice, you will show that you see teachers as competent, and you can help build their confidence to change.

Acknowledge and Validate

One of the most poignant reminders of the impact of acknowledging and validating is expressed in this quote by Parker Palmer: "We must remember this simple truth: the human soul does not want to be fixed, it wants simply to be seen and heard." When leaders acknowledge and validate, it helps to build strong relationships where teachers feel truly heard. The key is to be fully present during interactions to mirror back or paraphrase what the individual is saying. This is a judgment-free process. It is not necessary to express whether you agree or disagree with the person, only that you heard what they are saying from their perspective. These phrases are helpful in formulating the message you want to reflect back: "What I am hearing you say is . . ." "What you are telling me . . ." "I want to be sure I am understanding you clearly . . ."

The benefits of using a strengths-based approach can extend far beyond helping teachers achieve their stated goals. Teachers truly flourish in environments where they feel respected and acknowledged for their individual talents. The life-changing impact of strengths-based coaching was summarized in this handwritten note I received from a school leader: "I want you to know how grateful I am to have been given the opportunity to work with you. The impact on my professional life has been remarkable, but what I discovered was that coaching had an even greater impact on my personal life. I find myself looking for the positive in almost every situation, and then trying to find what I can do to make it better. So, thank you, Susan, for showing me the good in my work, my life, and in me."

The Art of Great Coaching

Spending time and energy on the development of effective coaching skills is a wise investment for leaders. If you embrace strengths-based coaching, you can add focused and supportive elements to your supervisory work with teachers. Clearly stating your professional goals related to coaching skills and identifying action steps in your IPDP will help. Consider the following ideas for improving your coaching skills:

- Start a book group with other school leaders. The resources list at the end of this chapter will give you some book ideas. The Colorado Coaching Consortium also provides a multitude of options on its website (http://www.cocoaches.net/CoachingResources.html).

- Attend workshops, courses, or conferences focused on coaching skills.

- Find a mentor with strong coaching skills to guide you as you develop your skills.

- Watch some of these powerful TED Talks:

    - "Do Schools Kill Creativity" by Sir Ken Robinson
      (https://www.ted.com/talks/ken_robinson_says_schools_kill_creativity)

    - "Your Body Language Shapes Who You Are" by Amy Cuddy
      (https://www.ted.com/talks/amy_cuddy_your_body_language_shapes_who_you_are)

    - "Playful Inquiry—Try this Anywhere" by Robyn Stratton Berkessel
      (http://tedxtalks.ted.com/video/Playful-Inquiry-Try-This-Anywhe;search%3Aappreciative)

- Explore coaching certification programs, such as these well-regarded programs:

    - Institute for Professional Excellence in Coaching (www.ipeccoaching.com)

    - Center for School Transformation—Evocative Coaching Training
      (www.centerforschooltransformation.com)

    - Horizons in Learning—Self-Paced Professional Development for Coaches
      (www.ConstantHine.com)

    - Thinking Collaboratively—Cognitive Coaching Seminars (http://www.thinkingcollaborative
      .com/seminars_cc_seminars/)

The International Coaching Federation has a complete listing of accredited training programs on its website (http://www.coachfederation.org).

When leaders fully commit to developing strengths-based coaching skills, they will be equipped to illuminate each teacher's strengths, no matter how dormant, and engage with their own strengths to successfully transform their areas of growth.

Reflective Practice Exercises

Strengths-based coaching scripts can provide a solid starting point for having meaningful dialogue with teachers regarding their professional talents and ideas for growth.

> *We have reached the end of problem solving as a mode of inquiry capable of inspiring, mobilizing and sustaining human system change. The future belongs to methods that affirm, compel, and accelerate learning while including the voices of all the people who will be affected by the change.*
>
> —David Cooperrider, Professor, Weatherhead School of Management,
> Case Western Reserve University

PAIRED INTERVIEW

1. We go through highs and lows in our professional lives. Thinking back on the last twelve months, reflect on a high-point moment—a time that is memorable and stands out when you felt most engaged or challenged, or gained an important insight about your strengths or talents. Please share the story.

   - What was the situation?

   - Who else was involved?

   - What were you doing?

   - What happened that made you more aware of your strengths?

   - How did it make you feel?

2. Let's imagine we ask three people (colleagues, parents, friends, past supervisors) who know you well to share the three best qualities they see in you. What do you imagine they would say?

3. Why would they pick those qualities?

4. Choose one of your strengths and remember a time when you fully lived up to that strength. What happened? How did working with that strength affect your engagement, productivity, and job satisfaction?

5. As you continuously seek to develop yourself, how will you generate your own inspiration?

- Which strengths will you develop further?

- How will you amplify your existing strengths?

- What possibilities can you imagine when you amplify your strengths?

- What excites you about using this strength in new ways?

Source: Adapted from: Stratton-Berkessel, Robyn. 2010. *Appreciative Inquiry for Collaborative Solutions: 21 Strength-Based Workshops.* San Francisco: Pfeiffer.

WRITE A COACHING PLATFORM

A coaching platform puts into words your hopes and intentions as a coach. It states clearly and concisely your understanding of the purpose of coaching as well as how you will use strengths-based coaching strategies in your daily work. When you write your platform, identify the basic values, beliefs, and ethical standards that will inform your coaching. Describe how you hope to enhance the professional development of the teachers or school leaders with whom you work.

COACHING SCRIPTS

These sample scripts will help you get started in using coaching to strengthen your supervisory work with teachers:

Supporting Goal Achievement

Story: Tell me about the key goal that you would like to achieve this year. How would achieving this goal benefit you as a professional educator and the children in your care?

Crystal ball: If you were able to look through a magical crystal ball and see your goal coming to life for you . . . What would you see? What would you hear? What would you feel? Describe a vision you have for your work at its most fulfilling.

Magic wand: If tonight before bed you could wave a magic wand and all aspects of your goal were accomplished . . . What would you notice when you arrive in your classroom? What would be different? What would you be doing? What would the children be doing? How would you feel? How would it affect the people you are working with? What ideas do you have for bringing this goal to life?

Let's brainstorm four to five small steps you could begin to take.

Let's work on developing SMART goals and action steps: specific, measurable, attainable, relevant, and time bound.

Which of these action steps could you begin to work on this week or month?

How comfortable are you with this plan on a scale of one to ten?

Facilitating Environmental Change

Story: Describe for me an environmental change that you would like to make to enhance the quality of your work environment. Where did the idea for this environmental change come from?

Remote control hover camera: If I were able to send my remote control hover camera into your work environment after this change has been made, and we sat down and reviewed the images together, what would we see? Hear? Feel?

Needs: Describe for me what specific needs this environmental change would meet for you. How would it benefit the children in your care?

Let's work together to design a plan that will help you bring this environmental change to life. What are three to four small SMART steps that would start this process?

How comfortable are you with this plan on a scale of one to ten?

Shifting Perspectives: Vantage Points and Pivot Points

Story: Share a story of joyous or challenging experiences you had while working with another person to a reach a goal.

Perspective: After you have shared your story, retell the story from the perspective of the other person you worked with (this is the vantage-point task) or try retelling the story after imagining how the experience might have turned out differently (this is the pivot-point task).

Reflect: Think about the different perspectives revealed by looking at the situation through a different lens. How did taking a different perspective enlighten you? What feelings did it bring up? What else did you learn from the experience?

CHAPTER 8

Embracing Change— Letting Go of the Status Quo

Never believe that a few caring people can't change the world. For indeed that's all who ever have.

–Margaret Mead, *The World Ahead: An Anthropologist Anticipates the Future*

Leaders in the early childhood field are facing a huge dilemma. On the one hand, they are expected to facilitate changes that reflect a continually evolving set of quality standards based on the growing body of research on how children learn. On the other hand, they are overwhelmed by the weight of constantly changing expectations and fear of embracing new ways of working. The result is resistance to moving away from the safety of the status quo.

Although the resistance to change can feel insurmountable to you as a leader, keep in mind that all significant changes are fraught with stressful emotions. Michael Fullan, in his book *Change Forces: Probing the Depths of Educational Reform*, acknowledges that the change process is somewhat unpredictable and volatile. But those who are skilled in change, he asserts, keep looking for ways to influence improvements that will help them get closer to their goals. He also notes that skilled change leaders are open to shifts in the target during the change process. As a school leader, you can encourage teachers to move past the common feeling that they are taking one step forward and two steps back.

If you can help educators in your program stay the course during the inevitable periods of frustration that mark times of change, they will be rewarded by the results of their focused, intentional work. Fullan describes the roller-coaster ride of change in this way: "The more accustomed one becomes to dealing with the unknown, the more one understands that creative breakthroughs are always preceded by periods of cloudy thinking, confusion, exploration, trial, and stress; followed by periods of excitement and growing confidence as one pursues purposeful change, or copes with unwanted change." Challenge teachers to keep moving forward, and applaud their progress.

Margie Carter aptly refers to the early childhood field's inability to embrace change as the TTWWADI Syndrome. Holding on to a "that's the way we've always done it" way of thinking prevents individuals and programs from moving forward. Lisa Lee, a program officer with First Five San Francisco Children and Families Commission, clearly and powerfully states why the early childhood field must move away from the TTWWADI mind-set: "Change is necessary to address our own tolerance for mediocrity. Change is essential to close the opportunity gap that exists for so many children and their families. And change is necessary to close the opportunity gap that has existed for many in our workforce."

The Urgent Need for Change

The need for transformational changes in our early childhood education programs has never been clearer. Each new study shows a widening gap between what we know about the importance of every aspect of early childhood education and what is actually happening in programs. The following quotes show the consensus around the need for change:

- "Today, it is time for every young child in America to have access to high-quality preschool. It is time that we level the playing field and stop playing catch-up."

  —U.S. Secretary of Education Arne Duncan at the
  U.S. Hispanic Chamber of Commerce Legislative Summit, March 19, 2013

- "The pattern of results over the first 30 years of life provides a clearer than ever scientific understanding of how early childhood education can be an important contributor to academic achievement and social competence in adulthood. The next major challenge is to provide high-quality early childhood education to all the children who need it and who can benefit from it."

  —Craig Ramey, Virginia Tech Carilion Research Institute, January 19, 2012

- "We still haven't found the will to ensure that all our children, especially the most vulnerable, have the early childhood opportunities they need. We owe our young children better. The gap between the rhetoric and the reality is stunning given the research, the support of our top economists, and the growing understanding of the importance of our children's earliest years not only for school success but for our nation's economic success."

—Helen Blank, National Women's Law Center,
at Wheelock College, Boston, May 24, 2012

- "Investing in high-quality child care and early education builds a strong foundation of cognitive and social skills in young children that can improve their engagement in school and increase per capita earnings and economic development. Business leaders and policymakers should consider investment in young children one of the most effective strategies to secure the future economic strength of their communities and the nation."

—Committee on Economic Development, "Unfinished Business:
Continued Investment in Child Care and Early Education
Is Critical to Business and America's Future," June 2012

- "I'm just convinced that if we can close achievement gaps before children enter kindergarten, we have a chance to close them forever."

—U.S. Education Secretary Arne Duncan,
responding to Facebook comments, August 3, 2011

- "Children who participate in [high-quality early childhood education] programs are more likely to have the necessary skills-such as abstract reasoning, problem solving and communication-to meet the demands of tomorrow's workforce."

—Robert Wood Johnson Foundation Commission to Build a Healthier America

It is well-established that high-quality programs have a lasting impact on children. So face your fear of change head on and fully embrace your role in providing quality learning environments for all children, families, and teachers.

Understanding Our Immunity to Change

Carlina Rinaldi eloquently expresses the magnitude of the challenges of innovation: "In my opinion, this is why true innovations are so difficult to accept and appreciate. They 'shake up' our frames of reference because they force us to look at the world with new eyes. They open us up to what is different and unexpected. We tend to accept the status quo, that which we know and have already tried out . . . even when it does not satisfy us, even when it makes us feel stressed, confused, and hopeless." Understanding why it is so hard to move beyond the status quo and why individuals and organizations are resistant to change can be illustrated with depth and clarity through the immunity to change (ITC) process.

The ITC process was developed by Harvard Graduate School of Education professors Robert Kegan and Lisa Lahey. The four-column Immunity to Change Map on page 121 creates a "mental map that functions something like an X-ray, a picture of the invisible made visible," Kegan and Lahey note. "The X-ray or immunity map helps us all to see not just how things are at the moment, but why they are this way, and what will actually need to change in order to bring about any significant new results." By uncovering and naming previously hidden big assumptions, people discover their own unique immune system that has been protecting them by preventing their fears from coming to life. This powerful process helps make sense of our deep attachment to the status quo and provides a new framework for examining and rethinking behaviors that are preventing growth and change.

A vivid example of the power of the immunity to change process is my work with Milena, an experienced early childhood director who was struggling to achieve her goal of providing strengths-based feedback and engaging with her staff around the development of meaningful individual professional development plans. Milena expressed a strong commitment to her goal but had been unsuccessfully trying to achieve it for eighteen months. She knew something was holding her back, but she could not clarify what it was. Together, we worked through the following steps to reveal her immunity to change.

Goal clarification: Milena was passionate about her goal to support the professional growth of her teachers and to find new ways to increase the teachers' investment in their IPDPs. After a couple of drafts, Milena found the language to express her goal in a way that felt powerful to her. See column one in the Align! box that follows.

Doing or not doing: Next it was time for Milena to acknowledge what she was doing or not doing that prevented her from achieving her goal. I encouraged her to honestly list specific behaviors (not emotions) that were undermining her progress. With some gentle prompting to make this list as comprehensive as possible, Milena had no trouble coming up with a lengthy list of exactly what she was doing that held her back from achieving her goal. See column two in the Align! box.

Hidden competing commitments: To reveal Milena's hidden competing commitments and build her understanding of why she was holding herself back from achieving her goals, we worked through two steps. First, I asked Milena to think about doing the exact opposite of everything that she listed in column two and then state what she would worry about. Reflecting on actually removing her own barriers to achieving her goals was an emotional process for Milena. She was able to list her fears in a way that she had not been able to verbalize before. The second part of this column was to convert her worries into active commitments that were holding her back from reaching her goal. I explained to her that her worries were part of a very powerful immune system that was actively protecting her from having her fears come true. She was a bit puzzled by this until I explained that her goal was like stepping on the gas in her car. Her fears were the hidden commitments that, like the brakes of the car, were preventing her from moving forward. I asked her to restate her worries into what she was actively committed to not happening. Her hidden commitments were summed up in two powerful statements that are listed at the bottom of column three in the Align! box.

Big assumptions: The last step in creating Milena's map was to clarify the big assumptions that were keeping her immune system intact. What were her inner beliefs that kept prompting her to step on the brakes? Milena's big assumptions made it perfectly clear why she was having such a challenging time achieving her goal. These big-time-bad beliefs were very real to Milena, and stating them clearly helped her to understand her own immunity to change. Milena's big assumptions are listed in column four in the Align! box.

Milena's Immunity to Change Map reflects the fears that are holding many leaders back from making the changes they want and need to make. The fear of being judged, criticized, or being seen as less than competent can keep leaders shuttered safely in their comfort zone. Kegan and Lahey explain: "The idea behind the immunity to change is that we do not merely have these fears; we sensibly, even artfully, protect ourselves from them. We create ways of dealing with the anxiety these fears provoke. We are not only afraid; we take action to combat our fears. We defend ourselves from what terrifies us. We are actively (but not necessarily consciously) committed to making sure the things we are afraid of do not happen."

Revealing these big assumptions is actually a pivotal turning point for breaking free of the previously hidden beliefs that prevent us from making changes. In Milena's case, looking at her map as an X-ray of her hidden commitments was both surprising and enlightening. She was immediately struck by the logic behind her own behaviors. Milena was constantly feeling disappointed in her own inability to achieve her goal and in herself for avoiding the important work of engaging with her staff around their IPDPs. Seeing that her powerful hidden commitments and big assumptions were actually in place to protect her from her own fears was eye-opening, to say the least. By identifying her own immune system through this insightful process, Milena was able to look at new ways to start taking her own foot off the brakes and achieve her goal.

The Journey Forward

Embracing change is a journey that takes time and persistence. Creating an immunity to change map reveals a new starting point for this journey. By discovering your own hidden commitments and big assumptions, it is possible to move past the self-protective behaviors that have been holding you back from reaching your goals.

Discovering Your Hidden Commitments and Assumptions

Milena's Immunity to Change Map

Commitment (Improvement Goal)	Doing or Not Doing (Instead of Commitment)	Hidden Competing Commitment	Big Assumptions
Criteria: —True for you —Implicates you —Room for improvement —Important to you Goal: To become a leader who provides nonjudgmental, inspiring and insightful feedback that supports each teacher and invites them to become fully engaged in the process of discovering their own strengths and professional development goals.	**Criteria:** —Behaviors (not emotions) that work against col. 1 —Not "why" or what you should do about it • Not maintaining boundaries • Not paying attention to their perspective • I don't follow through • Not always being honest, being too careful of hurt feelings, not being objective • Procrastination • Dealing with challenges and emergencies • Not finding the time and space • Putting off important conversations • Not delegating • Not staying positive and keeping the energy moving forward • Not taking care of myself • Being judgmental • Not letting staff go • Not keeping the goal in mind • Not setting realistic expectations	**Worries:** • Afraid of being the bad guy • I won't be perfect • They still won't be happy • I'm not going to please everyone • I was wrong • I will be judged for my actions • My work will not be good • They'll stop talking to me • It will cause chaos • I will have to keep doing it • That I might not be able to inspire my staff • Will I know enough? • I will lose respect **Criteria:** —Follows from the fear —Commitment to self-protection —Show why col. 2 behaviors make good sense! —You see the immune system, and it feels powerful I am committed to not letting people see me as less than competent. I am committed to maintaining the status quo so I wouldn't be judged or criticized.	**Criteria:** —See how it sustains immune system —Has a "big-time-bad" conclusion for you —Shows a bigger world for you ("I must not enter") • If I provide inspiring, constructive, and nonjudgmental feedback, then I could lose respect, create chaos, and damage the interpersonal relationships that I value. • If I commit to being a leader who provides inspiring, constructive and nonjudgmental feedback, then my staff will realize that I don't have the skills, knowledge, and confidence needed to do this job.

Source: Adapted from: Kegan, Robert, and Lisa Laskow Lahey. 2009. *Immunity to Change: How to Overcome It and Unlock Potential in Yourself and Your Organization.* Boston, MA: Harvard Business.

The ITC process includes specific activities that are useful in overturning your immune system. These exercises are not a quick fix; they require a willingness to stay focused on the process to increase your own awareness of how and when your big assumptions hold you back from achieving your goals. Use the following list of activities as a guide for overturning your unique immune system:

- **Create your immunity to change map.** Use the story of Milena's map as a guide for developing your map. Review and revise your map so that it feels powerful to you and meets the criteria listed at the top of each column. You can use the sample map in Appendix F.

- **Identify what success looks like.** Plan out your continuum of progress to create a clear picture of what success will look like when you have achieved your goal and overturned your big assumption. Start by listing the goal and big assumptions from the immunity to change map. Then describe what full success would look like for you. Once you have a vivid image of what full success would look like, write down the first steps you could take to achieve full success. Then note what significant progress would look like.

Continuum of Progress

Goal and Big Assumptions	First Steps Forward	Significant Progress	Success
Goal: Big Assumptions:			

Source: Adapted from: Kegan, Robert, and Lisa Laskow Lahey. 2009. *Immunity to Change: How to Overcome It and Unlock Potential in Yourself and Your Organization.* Boston, MA: Harvard Business.

- **Enhance the continuum of progress.** Create a vision board that visually captures what full success would look like for you. Having an inspiring vision of success will guide you on your journey to achieve your goals. (See the vision-board exercise in chapter 2.)

- **Increase your self-awareness.** It's important to tune in to when your big assumptions are affecting your behavior. Only then will you realize the influence they have on your ability to achieve your goals. Find time each day to conduct self-observations and reflect on when, where, and why your big assumption was activated.

- **Uncover the origin of your big assumption.** Understanding the history of your big assumptions can increase your awareness of the impact that they have on your life. Reflect on the origins of each big assumption: Where does it stem from? Is it still valid?

- **Test your big assumptions.** Try behaving in ways that contradict your big assumption. Reflect on how that makes you view your assumption. Try this several times. The purpose of your tests is to see what happens when you do not let your big assumption control your behavior. Each test will provide information about the validity of your big assumption.

- **Look at your continuum of progress.** Use an action from your list of first steps forward.

- **Review your hidden competing commitments.** Perform an action that runs counter to one of the commitments.

By investing time, energy and focus on understanding your own immune system it becomes possible to move forward to achieve your desired goals without constantly putting the brakes on your own progress. As Milena worked her way through each of these exercises, she realized that her big assumptions were not always true. Through a series of small tests, Milena saw that her staff valued her positive feedback and expertise as a leader in the field. Even more importantly, the test revealed to her that she was strengthening her relationships with her staff and building on the solid foundation of respect she had worked hard to establish. With this valuable data, Milena was able to get past her fears of creating chaos in her program and damaging relationships. She moved forward to develop new strategies for engaging with teachers around their professional development goals.

Embracing New Possibilities

The strategies outlined in this book provide guideposts for leaders to actively engage in the process of transforming the quality of early childhood programs. When leaders understand why moving beyond the status quo is so hard and why people and organizations resist change, true transformation is possible. Leading from a positive, strengths-based perspective represents a paradigm shift: a clear movement away from the traditional and habitual and often stagnant leadership practices toward fully engaged, intentional, and relational strategies. Together these eight interrelated strategies build on each other to create the upward spiral of positive, strengths-based energy needed for innovative, sustainable changes in program quality to occur.

Using these strategies, you can create an upward spiral of inspirational leadership fueled by creativity, passion, and full engagement. To successfully and gracefully guide your program into the next era of quality, you must willingly commit to continually developing your leadership skills and to actively incorporating new skills and strategies into your daily work. When leaders actively embrace new thoughts, ideas, research, and practices, you will move past the limiting role of maintaining the status quo and unlock a world of innovative possibilities for holistically enhancing all aspects of your program.

Eight Transformational Strategies

Strategy	How It Supports Sustainable Change
Create a vision	A compelling vision guides the transformation process by providing a clear purpose and an inspirational focus for the changes necessary to transform the future.
Infuse positive energy	Positive energy is vital to creating and sustaining strengths-based learning communities where strong relationships thrive and attaining positive learning outcomes is possible.
Develop purposeful individual professional development plans	Professional development plans, when completed through a collaborative process, create detailed and well-defined road maps to guide growth and positive change.
Engage in continuous quality improvement	The goals stated in program improvement plans guide leaders in how they prioritize their time, allocate resources, enhance curriculum, improve environments, strengthen instructional practices, and select meaningful professional development experiences.
Ignite passion through engaged leadership	Leaders who are passionate, intentional, and fully engaged will be able to facilitate the continuous quality improvements necessary to keep pace with the new standards and initiatives designed to improve child outcomes.
Facilitate effective professional development	Incorporating new learner-centered approaches to professional development will increase engagement and facilitate continuous growth and goal achievement.
Use strengths-based coaching techniques to increase engagement	Strengths-based coaching is a relationship-based professional development activity that produces significant positive benefits and outcomes for teachers, administrators, children, and families.
Embrace change: Let go of the status quo	Understanding why it is so hard to move beyond the status quo and why individuals and organizations are resistant to change are essential tasks for leaders to facilitate transformations in their program.

Reflective Practice Exercise

CREATE DIALOGUE AROUND THE CHANGE PROCESS

- Have two poster boards ready. Give each participant two different colors of sticky notes. Have them write a positive response or outcome to the proposed change on one sticky note and a frustration they are feeling or challenge they are facing on the other. Place all the positive responses on one poster board, and the frustrations and challenges on the other. Guide a discussion based on the responses.

- Ask the participants to divide into small groups and have them create a children's storybook that depicts the change that the program is going through. Provide a variety of papers, fasteners, markers, magazines (for illustrations), pens, pencils, and glue sticks. Give the group set times for planning the book and then for illustrating the book—up to thirty minutes for each activity. Have each group share their stories with the larger group. Facilitate a discussion around the common themes and messages about change.

APPENDIX A

Creating a Vision Statement to Ignite Passion, Intentionality, and Engagement

Vision Statement

Create a vision statement that accurately reflects your hopes and dreams for adding more positivity, joy, and engagement to your professional life. What are you committed to? How can you live more fully in the upward spiral? What will your ideal professional life look, feel, and be like in a year, two years, or five years?

_____

_____

_____

_____

_____

_____

_____

_____

Crafting Affirmation Statements

*We always attract into our lives whatever we think about
most, believe in most strongly, expect on the deepest level,
and imagine most vividly.*

—Shakti Gawain, *Creative Visualization: Use the Power
of Your Imagination to Create What You Want in Your Life*

Affirmations are positive statements that will help your goals become reality. Affirmations should be written in the present tense—as if you have already achieved the goal. Write your affirmation statements on index cards and place them where you can read them every day.

Examples:

- *I effectively use strength-based communication with the children, educators, and parents in my program.*
- *I focus my attention on meeting the needs of a child who is facing a challenge.*
- *I choose joy and happiness, and allow wonderful things to happen daily in my classroom.*

Clearly state your affirmations:

_____

_____

_____

_____

_____

APPENDIX C

Vision and Goals Summary

Complete this form using the information from your vision statement, IPDPs for administrators and teachers, and your program improvement plan. Keep this summary in a visible spot where you can review it often to keep your daily work aligned with the key goals.

Vision for Program

Goals for Program

-
-
-
-

Goals for Administrators

-
-
-
-

Goals for Teachers

-
-
-
-

APPENDIX D

Sample IPDP Summary Sheet

Review the IPDPs for all program staff and list their names and number of goals in each core competency (for example, Susan 2) to understand common individual professional development needs and how that might affect the overall program's needs. This example uses the Core Competencies for Early Education and Care and Out of School Time Educators provided by the Massachusetts Department of Early Education and Care. Adapt this form to reflect your own local standards. Use the completed summary sheet as a guide for planning staff meetings and professional development experiences for the staff that will address the identified needs.

Program	1. Understanding the Growth and Development of Children	2. Guiding and Interacting with Children	3. Partnering with Families and Communities	4. Health, Safety, and Nutrition
Administrators				
Infant				
Toddler				
Preschool				
School Age				

Program	5. Learning Environments and the Curriculum	6. Observation, Assessment, and Documentation	7. Program .lanning and Development	8. Professionalism and Leadership
Administrators				
Infant				
Toddler				
Preschool				
School Age				

Inspiring Early Childhood Leadership

Sample Professional Development Planning Sheet

Review and Reflect

Before completing this form review:

- The IPDP core competency summary

- The vision and goals summary

- Trainings required by QRIS, NAEYC, and licensing

Create a Professional Development Calendar

Include all dates of regular staff meetings and professional development days.

Topic	Presenter or In-House Facilitator	Link to Goals, QRIS, NAEYC, Licensing, Core Competencies	Date	Resources Needed

APPENDIX F

Your Immunity to Change Map

Name:_____ **Date:**_____

Commitment (Improvement Goals)	Doing or Not Doing Instead (Behaviors That Work against the Goals)	Hidden Competing Commitments	Big Assumptions
Criteria: —True for you —Implicates you —Room for improvement —Important to you	Criteria: —Behaviors (not emotions) that work against col. 1 —Not "why" or what you should do about it	Worries Criteria: —Follows from the fear —Commitment to self-protection —Show why col. 2 behaviors make good sense! —You see the immune system, and it feels powerful	Criteria: —See how it sustains immune system —Has a "big-time-bad" conclusion for you —Shows a bigger world for you ("I must not enter")

Adapted from: Kegan, Robert, and Lisa Laskow Lahey. 2009. *Immunity to Change: How to Overcome It and Unlock Potential in Yourself and Your Organization.* Boston, MA: Harvard Business. http://mindsatwork.com

Resources

Achor, Shawn. 2011. "The Happy Secret to Better Work." TED Talks. http://www.ted.com/talks/shawn_achor_the_happy_secret_to_better_work?language=en

Adelaide Thinker in Residence. 2012. "Carlina Rinaldi on Documentation." https://www.youtube.com/watch?v=hUVi-fLc0zA&list=PLCI-Ug-AfaL1RN3vTuaS5mtkXcFIlhS72

Adkins, Amy. 2016. "Employee Engagement in U.S. Stagnant in 2015." Gallup. http://www.gallup.com/poll/188144/employee-engagement-stagnant-2015.aspx

Barnett, W. Steven. 2004. "Better Teachers, Better Preschools: Student Achievement Linked to Teacher Qualifications." *Preschool Policy Matters* (2). New Brunswick, NJ: National Institute for Early Education Research.

Black, David S. 2011. "A Brief Definition of Mindfulness." *Mindfulness Research Guide,* accessed May 14, 2016. http://citeseerx.ist.psu.edu/viewdoc/download?doi=10.1.1.362.6829&rep=rep1&type=pdf

Bloom, Paula Jorde. 2014. *Leadership in Action: How Effective Directors Get Things Done.* Lake Forest, IL: New Horizons.

Bloom, Paula Jorde. 2015. *Blueprint for Action: Leading Your Team in Continuous Quality Improvement* (3rd ed.). Lake Forest, IL: New Horizons.

Canfield, Jack. 2015. "Seven Steps for Creating the Life You Want." Web log post, accessed January 15, 2015. http://jackcanfield.com/7-steps-for-creating-the-life-you-want/

Carter, Margie. 2003. "Supervising or Coaching—What's the Difference." *Child Care Information Exchange*: 20–22.

Carter, Margie, and Lisa Lee. 2015, March-April. "Are We Suffering from TTWWADI Syndrome?" *Exchange,* 24–27.

Center for the Study of Social Policy. 2016. "Strengthening Families Self-Assessment Tool for Center-Based Early Care and Education Programs," accessed May 14, 2016. http://www.cssp.org/reform/strengtheningfamilies/2014/CENTER-BASED-EARLY-CARE-AND-EDUCATION-PROGRAM-SELF-ASSESSMENT.pdf

Chapman, Gary D., and Paul E. White. 2011. *The Five Languages of Appreciation in the Workplace: Empowering Organizations by Encouraging People.* Chicago: Northfield.

Connette, Earle. 1938. "A Questionnaire for Supervisors." *Music Educators Journal* 24(3): 19.

Covey, Stephen, A. Roger Merrill, and Rebecca Merrill. 1994. *First Things First.* New York: Free Press.

Cuddy, Amy. 2012. "Your Body Language Shapes Who You Are." TED Talks. http://www.ted.com/talks/amy_cuddy_your_body_language_shapes_who_you_are

Dewey, John. 1910. *How We Think*. Lexington MA: D.C. Heath.

Diaz-Maggioli, Gabriel. 2004. *Teacher-Centered Professional Development*. Alexandria, VA: ASCD.

Drago-Severson, Ellie. 2008. "Four Practices Serve as Pillars for Adult Learning." *National Staff Development Council* 29(4): 60–63.

Fredrickson, Barbara. 2009. *Positivity*. New York: Crown.

Feinberg, Cara. 2010. "The Mindfulness Chronicles: On the Psychology of Possibility." *Harvard Magazine* (September-October 2010): 42–45.

Fullan, Michael. 1993. *Change Forces: Probing the Depth of Educational Reform*. London: Falmer.

Fullan, Michael. 1993. "Why Teachers Must Become Change Agents." *Educational Leadership* 50(6): 12–18.

Gandini, Lella. 1991. "Not Just Anywhere: Making Child Care Centers into 'Particular' Places," *Child Care Information Exchange*: 5–9.

Gordon, Jon. 2007. *The Energy Bus: 10 Rules to Fuel Your Life, Work, and Team with Positive Energy*. Hoboken, NJ: Wiley.

Helterbran, Valeri R., and Beatrice S. Fennimore. 2004. "Collaborative Early Childhood Professional Development Building from a Base of Teacher Investigations." *Early Childhood Educational Journal* 31(4): 267–271.

Hoerr, Thomas R. 1996. "Introducing the Theory of Multiple Intelligences." *NASSP Bulletin* 80(583): 8.

International Coach Federation. 2011. *Core Competencies*. http://www.coachfederation.org/icfcredentials/core-competencies/

Jones, Dewitt. n.d. *Celebrate What's Right With the World—Resources and Preview of Film*. http://www.celebratewhatsright.com

Katz, Lilian G. 1972. "Developmental Stages of Preschool Teachers." *ERIC Clearinghouse on Early Childhood Education*, Urbana, IL.

Kabat-Zinn, Jon. 2012. *Mindfulness for Beginners: Reclaiming the Present Moment—and Your Life*. Boulder, CO: Sounds True.

Kantrowitz, Barbara, and Pat Wingert. 1991. "The Ten Best Schools in the World." *Newsweek*, December 2.

Kegan, Robert, and Lisa Laskow Lahey. 2009. *Immunity to Change: How to Overcome It and Unlock Potential in Yourself and Your Organization*. Boston, MA: Harvard Business.

Kennedy, Anne, and Anne Stonehouse. 2012. *Victorian Early Years Learning and Development Framework: Practice Principle Guide 8 Reflective Practice*. Melbourne, Australia: State of Victoria Department of Early Childhood Education. http://www.education.vic.gov.au/Documents/childhood/providers/edcare/practiceguide8.PDF

Kieves, Tama. 2012. *Inspired and Unstoppable: Wildly Succeeding in Your Life's Work*. London: Tarcher/Penguin.

Lower, Joanna K., and Deborah J. Cassidy. 2007. "Child Care Work Environments: The Relationship with Learning Environments," *Journal of Research in Childhood Education* 22(2): 189–204.

Marturano, Janice. 2014. *Finding the Space to Lead: A Practical Guide to Mindful Leadership*. New York: Bloomsbury.

National Association for the Education of Young Children. 2015. *Using NAEYC Family and Teaching Staff Surveys*. Washington, DC. NAEYC. http://www.naeyc.org/academy/files/academy/Accreditation%20Update%20(2).pdf

National Association for the Education of Young Children. 2016. *NAEYC Early Childhood Program Standards and Accreditation Criteria and Guidance for Assessment.* Washington, DC. NAEYC. http://www.naeyc.org/academy /files/academy/Standards%20and%20Accreditation%20Criteria%20%26%20Guidance%20for %20Assessment_04.2016_1.pdf

National Association for the Education of Young Children, National Association of Child Care Resource and Referral Agencies. 2011. "Early Childhood Education Professional Development: Training and Technical Assistance Glossary." Washington, DC: NAEYC.

National Scientific Council on the Developing Child. 2007. *The Science of Early Childhood Development.* http://www.developingchild.net

Obama, Barack. 2013. "President's State of the Union Address." https://www.whitehouse.gov/the-press-office/2013/02 /12/president-barack-obamas-state-union-address

Office of Child Care's National Child Care Information Center, Information and Technical Assistance Center. 2010. "RBPD: TA Approaches and Research." Washington, DC: Administration for Children and Families.

Osterman, Karen F., and Robert B. Kottkamp. 1993. *Reflective Practice for Educators: Improving Schooling through Professional Development.* Newbury Park, CA: Corwin.

Palmer, Parker J. 1998. *The Courage to Teach: Exploring the Inner Landscape of a Teacher's Life.* San Francisco, CA: Jossey-Bass.

Palmer, Parker J., and Megan Scribner. 2007. *The Courage to Teach Guide for Reflection and Renewal.* San Francisco: Jossey-Bass.

Rinaldi, Carlina. 2006. *In Dialogue with Reggio Emilia: Listening, Researching and Learning.* London: Routledge.

Rinaldi, Carlina. 2012. "The Pedagogy of Listening: The Listening Perspective from Reggio Emilia." In *The Hundred Languages of Children: The Reggio Emilia Experience in Transformation,* edited by Carolyn P. Edwards, Lella Gandini, and George E. Forman, 233–246. Santa Barbara, CA: Praeger.

Robinson, Ken. 2006. "Do Schools Kill Creativity?" TED Talks. https://www.ted.com/talks/ken_robinson_says_schools _kill_creativity

Rush, Dathan D., and M'Lisa L. Shelden. 2011. *The Early Childhood Coaching Handbook.* Baltimore, MD: Paul H. Brookes.

Salzman, Julie Bayer, and Josh Salzman. 2015. "Just Breathe." YouTube video, 3:41. https://www.youtube.com /watch?v=RVA2N6tX2cg&index=5&list=FL0xom02vUsue1py8b0eBfjA

Schneider, Bruce D. 2008. *Energy Leadership: Transforming Your Workplace and Your Life from the Core.* Hoboken, NJ: Wiley.

Seale, Alan. 2003. *Soul Mission, Life Vision: Recognize Your True Gifts and Make Your Mark in the World.* Boston, MA: Red Wheel.

Seidal, Steve. 2008. "Foreward: Lessons from Reggio." In *Insights and Inspirations from Reggio Emilia.* Worcester, MA: Davis Publications.

Smith, Linda K. 2013. "BUILDing Strong Foundations: Continuous Quality Improvement: QRIS Is a Tool." http://buildinitiative.org/TheIssues/BUILDingStrongFoundations/tabid/223/PostID/8/Default.aspx

Stevens, Nicola. 2005. *Learn to Coach: The Skills You Need to Coach for Personal and Professional Development.* Oxford, UK: How to Books.

Stratton-Berkessel, Robyn. 2010. *Appreciative Inquiry for Collaborative Solutions: 21 Strength-Based Workshops*. San Francisco: Wiley.

Stratton-Berkessel, Robyn. 2014. "Playful Inquiry—Try this Anywhere." http://tedxnavesink.com/project/robyn-stratton-berkessel-2/

Sugarman, Nancy. 2011. "Putting Yourself in Action: Individual Professional Development Plans." *Young Children* 66(3): 27–33.

Talan, Teri, and Paula Jorde Bloom. 2011. *Program Administration Scale*, 2nd ed. New York: Teachers College Press.

Tarlov, Alvin R., and Michelle Precourt Debbink. 2008. *Investing in Early Childhood Development: Evidence to Support a Movement for Educational Change*. New York: Palgrave MacMillan.

Toogood, Kathy. 2012, June. "Strengthening Coaching: An Exploration of the Mindset of Executive Coaches Using Strengths-Based Coaching." *International Journal of Evidence Based Coaching and Mentoring*, Special Issue No. 6: 72–87.

Tschannen-Moran, Bob, and Megan Tschannen-Moran. 2010. *Evocative Coaching: Transforming Schools One Conversation at a Time*. San Francisco: Jossey-Bass.

Tschannen-Moran, Bob, and Megan Tschannen-Moran. 2011. "The Coach and the Evaluator." *Educational Leadership* 69(2): 10–16.

Ueland, Brenda. 1993. *Strength to Your Sword Arm: Selected Writings*. Duluth, MN: Holy Cow.

Waddell, Martin, and Jennifer Eachus. 1994. *The Big Big Sea*. Cambridge, MA: Candlewick.

Whitney, Diana Kaplin, Amanda Trosten-Bloom, and Kae Rader. 2010. *Appreciative Leadership: Focus on What Works to Drive Winning Performance and Build a Thriving Organization*. New York: McGraw-Hill.

Wiseman, Liz. 2013. *The Multiplier Effect: Tapping the Genius inside Our Schools*. Thousand Oaks, CA: Corwin.

Zakaria, Fareed. 2014. "Upward Mobility: Obama's Plan to Expand Pre-K Is a Step in a Long Catch-Up Game." *Time*, March 4. http://content.time.com/time/magazine/article/0,9171,2136877,00.html

Zepeda, Sally Jo. 2004. "Annotated Bibliography on Performance Coaching for Georgia's Leadership Institute for School Improvement." Atlanta: Georgia's Leadership Institute for School Improvement.

Index